Step into the Spotlight

Present with impact, inspire
confidence and get results

Russell Pickering

Published by TPG Publishing

First published in 2021 in Auckland, New Zealand

Copyright © Russell Pickering

www.thepickeringgroup.com

Auckland, New Zealand

Edited by Jenny Magee

Design by Extended Whānau

Illustrations by Ezra Whittaker-Powley

Printed by Print House, Hamilton, New Zealand

ISBN: 978-0-473-59948-5 (paperback)

ISBN: 978-0-473-59949-2 (ebook)

For Andrew

Contents

Introduction   1

From Evasion to Inspiration

Chapter One   The Trouble with Speaking   13
Chapter Two   The Archetypes of
                   Organisational Speakers   21
Chapter Three   Getting the Brief   43

Section I: Planning

Chapter Four   The Audience – Point A   59
Chapter Five   Your Objective – Point B   69
Chapter Six   The Structure   79

Section II: Messaging

Chapter Seven   The Open and Close   95
Chapter Eight   Your Core Content   107
Chapter Nine   Visual Aids   121

Section III: Delivery

Chapter Ten   Practise   139
Chapter Eleven   Courage   149
Chapter Twelve   Connect   163

                   Afterword   183
                   About the Author   185
                   Endnotes   186
                   Praise for Step into the Spotlight   191

Introduction

Congratulations on deciding to step into the spotlight and become a more confident, persuasive and compelling presenter. If you work in a business or organisation and are looking for a straightforward method to ensure you can craft and deliver impactful presentations, in-person and virtually, that inform, motivate and inspire, then this book is for you.

Let's kick things off with two undeniable (and potentially uncomfortable) facts.

It is the communication and execution of great ideas that propel our businesses and organisations forward. But oddly, we pay more attention and give more credence to those who project confidence – regardless of the quality of their ideas.

The result? Far too many promising careers stall, and great ideas fail to connect because of poor presentation skills. What's more, far too many bad ideas get adopted (and narcissistic leaders get promoted) because of our bias toward displays of confidence. The science is clear – we readily mistake confidence for competence. Yet, there is scant evidence to show that high confidence correlates to great leadership. In fact, the opposite may be true.[1]

Here's the thing. If you believe your ideas are of value – speak up! You have a duty to those ideas, your organisation, and possibly the world to ensure your ideas are heard.

This book is designed to help you do just that.

And yes, you can learn – but you better believe it!

I've been privileged to work in many organisations across New Zealand and Australia for more than fifteen years, helping thousands of people become better presenters. Whether in a sprawling government ministry, a large multi-national, a glass-towered professional services firm or a hip young start-up, the simple factor that differentiates presenters who consistently improve from those who struggle is the underlying belief that they can.

Stanford University Professor and motivation research pioneer Carol Dweck calls this a growth mindset – believing you can develop your skills and talents through hard work and feedback. The opposite of growth is a fixed mindset – believing your skills are innate and unchangeable.[2] Presenters who manage to master their challenges and consistently improve have a growth mindset. They understand that their skills are like muscles that become stronger if trained and developed. They also understand that *how* you train matters.

Focus on the core

A personal trainer at any good gym will tell you that real strength always starts with the core – neglect it at your peril. The same is true for presentations. Everything should begin with a clear and relevant core message. Get that right, and confidence in delivery will often take care of itself.

But if you think that all you need for impact are powerful delivery skills and inherent charisma, you're mistaken. Your manager may even reinforce this myth by telling you to 'Be more confident' or 'Just own the room.'

You wouldn't believe the number of phone calls I get from worried team leads that go something like this:

'We need you to come in and work with [insert name] on their presenting skills. They're really struggling to make an impact. The issue's not with their content – that's sorted – it's more to do with their delivery. We just need them not to suck.'

In the majority of cases, the issue is *always* content related. Content that's irrelevant, too dense, has too many slides, is unfamiliar, or all the above. Once that's sorted – boom, they're away!

I'm not saying delivery skills aren't essential. They are. (And don't worry, we'll talk about good delivery in later chapters.) But obsessing over them will distract you from where your real power comes from – your authenticity and your relevance. You do not need to be a performer or even an extrovert to be a great presenter, and anyone who tells you so is giving misguided advice. You are not there to entertain. Your purpose is to be of value to your audience, not to be evaluated by them.

In my experience, the most interesting and persuasive presenters deliver their message in a way that feels like a conversation they're having *with* me rather than a performance *for* me. Sure, they may inhabit a heightened version of themselves, with energy appropriate for their presentation context, but they are themselves, nonetheless. They own who they are. They seem comfortable in their skin. And the best part? Their message resonates and lingers in my mind long after the encounter because it's relevant to me. So, here's your first tip – start with something worth saying.

You might ask, 'Do I need to put myself out there? I just present marketing reports!'

YES! We need you. And we need your ideas to be communicated well – regardless of how mundane they may seem. If you're into a higher sense of purpose, let me share mine with you. Bear with me. I may get a bit ranty.

Things are out of whack

Look around. If you haven't noticed, the world is in a perilous state. Sure, it's 'the age of ideas', but there is a real risk that the weight of those ideas will favour the loudest rather than the best. Tectonic shifts are happening in the way we work. Big data, automation, machine learning, and artificial intelligence are creating massive labour market disruption. Vast, powerful digital communication platforms sold on the promise of connection with our fellow humans are doing the exact opposite. Despite their undeniable benefits, they've become algorithmic amplifiers of our own bias and outrage, fuelling the spread of disinformation and fear.

Meanwhile, global trust in business, government and science is collapsing. Add COVID-19, inequality, and the climate crisis into the mix and stir it all up with a rapid news, or rather, *entertainment* cycle that champions celebrity and opinion over considered, balanced debate and the world quickly begins to look decidedly precarious.

Arming the resistance

To navigate this chaos, we desperately need to hear every voice, not just the loudest. Too often, the charismatics, the bombastics, the braggadocios, the narcissists, the spin doctors, the loudmouths, the demagogues, the tricksters, and the flat-out liars dominate the conversation.

They've given the art of speaking a bad name – shifting it toward force and manipulation – and they've been celebrated and even worshipped for displays of brutal confidence over quiet competence. To restore balance, we need the quiet, the considered, the ethical, the authentic, the thoughtful and the kind amongst you to step forward in your businesses and organisations; competent and persuasive, equipped with the ability to communicate ideas that inspire us with a sense of meaning, belonging and purpose. Don't wait for a sympathetic ear. We need you right now. This is your time to step out of the shadows, into the spotlight and shine. Everything that we do at The Pickering Group supports people to do just that.

Ok, rant over.

If you're looking for motivation to improve that's a little more Jeremy Clarkson than Greta Thunberg, how about this: Get good at presenting and you'll likely earn more money, get promoted, and won't lose your job to a machine.

The reality

Good presenting skills are a critical part of leadership, whatever your level. They underpin your ability to communicate effectively, which in turn drives up team engagement and, ultimately, organisational performance. It is a skill that is increasingly critical in today's knowledge economy – consequently, those who demonstrate good persuasive speaking skills are generally more recognised and rewarded within an organisation.[3]

As an example, take a computer engineer in New Zealand's growing tech industry who only has technical coding skills. Their salary might start around $60,000. That same engineer who can confidently present to clients, sell their ideas to management and motivate their team to action can command upwards of $120,000.

According to recent research from persuasion and communication expert Carmine Gallo, your ability to *change minds* is the single greatest skill that will set you apart in the coming decade.[4]

Recent data from LinkedIn reinforces this trend showing persuasion as the second most in-demand soft-skill in 2019 and 2020.[5] In late 2018, LinkedIn CEO Jeff Weiner shared research from their comprehensive study of skills gaps in the workforce. It showed that the number one skills gap was soft skills. Of the 1.6 million people surveyed who lacked in this area, sixty-two per cent required oral communication skills. Weiner further concluded that people with strong communication skills are at far less risk of being replaced by emerging technology such as artificial intelligence.[6] As Gallo notes, it's clear that presenting skills should no longer be called 'soft' – they're fundamental.[7]

Dealing with Donald

For some of you, the idea of presenting persuasively may have an 'ick' factor to it.

Recently I was talking with a long-standing client who is a senior partner in a professional services firm. Her leadership team were struggling to pull themselves out of the detail, simplify their messaging and sell their ideas with conviction, but there was pushback when they heard she was about to put them through my advanced presenting programme. They recognised they weren't doing well, but were wary of the perceived sliminess of persuasive speaking skills. They were genuinely worried they would turn from considered, evidence-based experts into Donald Trump!

To be fair, they're right to be a little cautious. The line between persuasion and manipulation can be blurry. However, my response was this: Presenting persuasively need not come at the sacrifice of your authenticity or credibility. Rather, it should be strengthened by it. If you whole-heartedly believe that what you're communicating is of real value to your audience (and if you don't, then that should be ethically troubling), why wouldn't you want to be more effective? Wouldn't it be selfish to keep your ideas indecipherable?

Right then, let's crack into it.

What we'll cover

This book is a practical how-to guide to crafting and delivering impactful presentations and it's written in four parts.

Part One is all about context. In this section, I'll outline some of the unique challenges you face when presenting within organisations. I'll introduce the Archetypes of Organisational Speakers and the Three Practices of Presenting – Planning, Messaging and Delivery. These practices are the key to the spotlight and form the core of this book.

Parts Two, Three and Four unpack the Three Practices in turn. By the end, you will have a straightforward, efficient process that will ensure all your presentations (in-person and virtual) are relevant, compelling, and inspire confidence.

How to read this book

My advice? Read the whole book through first. It's a quick and easy read. Then, when your next presentation is approaching, allow yourself plenty of time to download the presentation canvas and structure template from our website www.thepickeringgroup.com/stepintothespotlight

Open this book at Chapter Four and follow the Quick Tips summarised in the yellow box at the end of each chapter. You can delve into each chapter for more detailed advice and examples, should you need them. Why not commit right now to doing this for your next presentation? You'll be amazed at the result. Do it often enough, and the process will become second nature. At that point, you won't need this book so pass it onto somebody who does. Or better yet, buy them their own copy!

Let's begin

I have one last piece of advice before we continue. Great presenting is not about you or your ego. It is selfless and an act of service. At its simplest, it's about respect – for an idea *and* an audience. You are merely the intermediary that connects them. Hold onto that idea of being of service. It will release you from anxiety and give you the freedom to explore.

So, draw on your courage and let's find your spotlight.

From Evasion
to Inspiration

Chapter One

The Trouble with Speaking

Presenting in a business or organisational context is uniquely challenging and very different from other forms of public speaking, where your focus may be more ceremonial or entertaining – such as delivering a speech at your best friend's wedding. What follows here are common challenges my clients tell me they face. How many of these have you mastered? More importantly, how many still master you?

The challenges of presenting

Inspiring confidence

Confidence is the biggest issue I get asked about. At some point, most of us have had well-meaning colleagues or managers say, '*Just be more confident*' – as though it's a switch you turn on. This approach is unhelpful because we hear, '*You look weak and timid*', which triggers self-consciousness.

Let's consider confidence in two ways: the confidence we have in ourselves and the confidence our audience has in us. If we obsess too much about trying to manufacture confidence, we risk becoming overly performative, taking us away from our authenticity and disconnecting us from our audience. We feel like an impostor. Instead, think of confidence as a feeling our audience has in us. Regardless of our worries, our audience is more likely to adopt our ideas or be persuaded by our arguments if we inspire confidence in them. They don't need to know what's going on inside our heads. So rather than obsessing over your confidence, draw on your courage. Courage trumps confidence. In fact, I think courage is so powerful that I've devoted a whole chapter to it.

Managing anxiety

There's a famous quote attributed to Mark Twain: 'There are two types of speakers: Those who get nervous and those who are liars.'

Any great speaker will tell you that nerves come with the territory. How then do they manage to make it look so easy? For many people, speaking anxiety may be so crippling that it is career limiting. The mere thought of an approaching presentation or important client meeting means a churning stomach and sleepless nights.

Then comes the delivery, where unmanaged anxiety means you're flooded with unhelpful amounts of adrenaline and cortisol – natural chemicals produced in response to a perceived threat. These chemicals play havoc with our ability to stay connected to our audience and often lead to unhelpful physiological reactions. Some of the most common include mind-blanks, a quavering voice, excessive sweating, shaking or trembling, shuffling or pacing, excessive filled pauses (ums and ahs), and difficulty making eye contact. We think, 'Maybe it's just safer to read my slides rather than risk losing my way and looking stupid.'

All these reactions distract an audience from our message. They notice us – but for all the wrong reasons. The uncomfortable truth is that audiences are heavily biased towards displays of confidence and judge your competence based on those displays.[1] Excessive external behaviours that signal timidity and nervousness may lead an audience to lose faith in you and your ideas, making you struggle to be noticed or heard. Worse still, more dominant colleagues may claim credit for your ideas.

To start with, don't worry about trying to conquer your fear. I've been in front of audiences for most of my life and still get nervous – sometimes awfully so. I've never learned how to conquer my nerves completely, and trust me, I've tried. Instead, I've learned how to accept them and keep them in check – well, most of the time.

Creating messages that resonate

If our messages and ideas fall flat and fail to connect, it is likely they are detailing what matters to us rather than focussed on what matters to our audience. The consequence? Anything from boredom or indifference to confusion and disengagement.

The foundation of a great presentation is empathy. Demonstrating that you truly understand your audience's needs, fears, frustrations, desires, hopes and dreams, opens them up to your ideas. As Dale Carnegie notes in his classic book on interpersonal persuasion, *How to Win Friends and Influence People*, 'You are interested in what you want...the rest of us are just like you: we are interested in what we want. So the only way on earth to influence other people is to talk about what *they* want and show them how to get it.'[2]

Speaking off-the-cuff

At times your ability to prepare is limited by factors out of your control. Perhaps you have to present on behalf of someone at short notice, or poor event organisation means the audience you expected bears no resemblance to those who have turned up. Or maybe a colleague, running a workshop for their team, asks you – on the day – to 'share a few words of encouragement on implementing the new strategy.'

In my experience, few people find off-the-cuff speaking easy. Most dread it and try their best to avoid it. However, you may be missing out on opportunities to build relationships and cultivate a reputation for openness and generosity.

Influencing up

Undoubtedly, the stakes are higher when you present to an audience with more status or power than you. Getting it right matters, and there are reputational risks to performing poorly. What's more, it's easy to become defensive when challenged. We can confuse robust questioning of our ideas with criticism of our intelligence or competence. There is, however, a positive flipside. Regardless of whether you win them over, remaining calm and present under pressure can do wonders for your reputation, and allows senior leaders to view your competence and build trust in your abilities. And that ties in with the next challenge.

Handling tough questions and holding your ground

There's nothing worse than an unexpected broadside that leaves you dumbstruck and stumbling for a reply. The adrenaline surges, your face flushes and the right words fail to emerge from your constricted throat. Other people in the room squirm, and maybe someone comes to your rescue – which makes you feel even worse. You leave the encounter and collect yourself, flooded with witty retorts you wish you'd thought of earlier.

However, delivering great answers is a huge credibility builder. In fact, as the status and power of your audience increases, so does the importance of nailing their questions. As anyone who has presented to a board or executive team will tell you, you'll be lucky to get through your first slide without being interrupted.

Turning complex data and analysis into compelling insight

Data is everywhere. Less abundant, though, are people with the skills to communicate that data as insight and story. As organisational development expert Josh Bersin notes, 'Today, for anyone who wants a shot at a well-compensated position...comfort with data is increasingly essential.'[3] Data, which is essentially a numerical account of the past, needs to be analysed, interpreted and then explained in a way that enables us to make better decisions for the future.[4]

Many of us opt for the dreaded data dump, presenting our audience with complicated spreadsheets and charts, facts and figures. One of my clients vividly describes this style of presenting as 'show up and throw up.' Ideas get lost in detail, time is wasted, attention spans are challenged, and the risk of bad decisions grows exponentially.

Using stories to engage, persuade and inspire

If you're not actively and comfortably using stories in your presentations, you're missing the most powerful tool available to connect with hearts and change minds. Yet, for many presenters, the skill of using stories to engage remains elusive or intimidating, so they continue to overburden audiences with information that has no emotional resonance. The primary result? The information lacks impact and is quickly forgotten.

Constructing visual aids that reinforce your message, not detract from it

After years of being subjected to death-by-PowerPoint, you would think that we would finally understand that simple, clear, uncluttered visual aids are far more powerful than dense documents, spreadsheets, or charts projected on a screen.

You'd also hope we'd understand the critical difference between a document and a visual aid. Alas, not yet. Too often, slides are read word-for-word, as if the audience cannot read for themselves. Many presenters still hide their subject matter insecurities or lack of preparation behind needlessly complicated slide decks that double as documents for the audience to take away. The result is wasted time, obfuscated meaning, and ideas that lack any action or purpose other than to inform.

'If all you want to do is create a file of facts and figures, cancel the meeting and email a report.' Thanks, Seth Godin.

Effective preparation with limited time

The reality of work is that many of us don't feel we have the luxury of time when preparing for our speaking encounters. With so much going on each day, and so many competing priorities, carving out time to research, construct and practise adequately seems inefficient, even indulgent. Unfortunately, poor preparation leads to unnecessary complications and murky thinking.

The French philosopher and mathematician Blaise Pascal famously wrote: 'I would have written a shorter letter, but I did not have the time.' It's easy to be complicated. Distilling your ideas into a simple, actionable message is far more challenging. An inescapable rule of thumb is that the quality of your presentation is always proportionate to the time you spend in preparation. And that includes practising.

Maintaining engagement when presenting virtually

American presentation guru Nancy Duarte said it best: 'What's worse than sitting through a really bad presentation? Sitting through a bad one delivered remotely.'

More than ever, workplaces all over the world are relying heavily on virtual communication. Speaking our ideas with clarity and confidence can be difficult enough without the challenge of doing so in a virtual environment. Added complications include: maintaining team cohesion and engagement, combatting 'Zoom' or virtual screen fatigue, poor microphone quality and camera set-up, adjusting content to be 'virtual-appropriate,' unstable internet connections and fatigued or distracted audiences. Nevertheless, virtual presenting is here to stay, and your job is to make it work for your ideas and your audience.

The three practices of presenting

The question we now face is how to master these challenges. Well, there's good news. There is a clear commonality across all who consistently do just that and step in their spotlight as presenters. They have developed a high level of competency across the following three practices of presenting: Planning, Messaging and Delivery. Mastering each practice is your pathway to the Spotlight. In Parts Two, Three and Four we'll unpack each practice in detail.

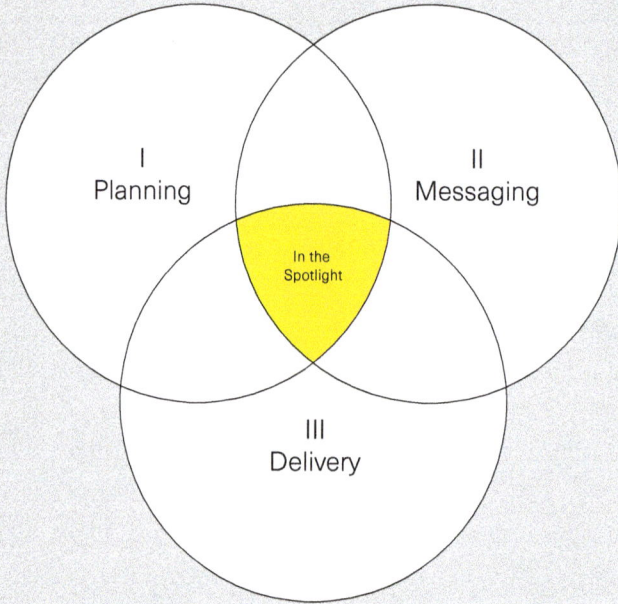

Figure 1: The three practices of presenting

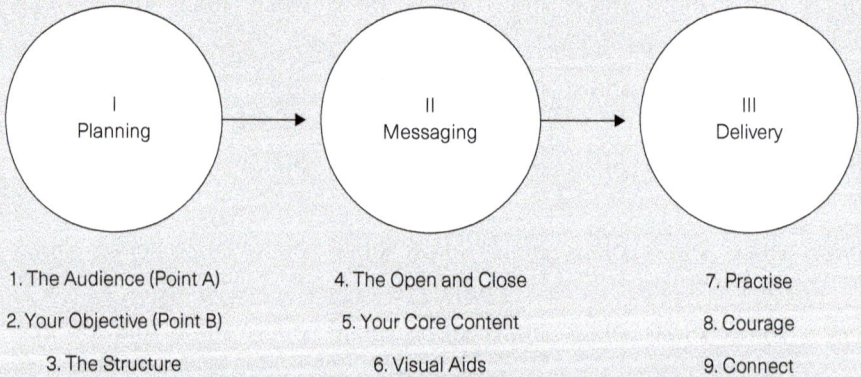

1. The Audience (Point A)
2. Your Objective (Point B)
3. The Structure

4. The Open and Close
5. Your Core Content
6. Visual Aids

7. Practise
8. Courage
9. Connect

Figure 2: Elements of the three practices

Chapter Two

The Archetypes of Organisational Speakers

Whitikina koe e te rā, ko tō atārangi ka mahue ki muri.
May the sun shine upon you and cast your shadows behind you.
Māori proverb

I've observed thousands of presenters in action over the past fifteen years – from the fearful to the fabulous and everywhere in between. Over that time, I've noticed behavioural patterns that either enhance or reduce a presenter's impact. These emerge as presenters try to overcome the challenges described in the previous chapter. Importantly, however, once a struggling presenter finds a reliable process to master these challenges, their impact instantly changes for the better. These patterns inspired my Archetypes of Organisational Speakers.

Archetype, you say?

The word archetype comes from the Greek term *archetypos* meaning original pattern. In literature, the term refers to a typical and recognisable character or storyline that repeatedly appears over time and even across different cultures – for example, the innocent child, noble hero or the wise sage. Most important to our understanding of archetypes is the concept of collective familiarity. To work well, archetypes must carry a universal meaning that is instantly recognisable and relatable. From the ancient Greeks like Plato and Theophrastus to psychologist Carl Jung's archetypes of our collective unconscious, familiar characters have helped us see universal patterns of meaning woven into the fabric of the human condition.

The inspiring idea

Before we go any further, I want to introduce you to master vocal coach, author and theatre practitioner Patsy Rodenburg. Her name will likely be unfamiliar, but you'll have heard of some of the people she's coached: Dame Judi Dench, Sir Ian McKellan, Nicole Kidman, Hugh Jackman, Daniel Day-Lewis, to name a few.

Rodenburg's teachings hugely influenced my development as a professional actor and now as a presentation coach and trainer. Her Three Circles of Energy [1] inspired part of the frame that underpins The Archetypes of Organisational Speakers, so I think it best to start with a brief overview of how her model functions.

Rodenburg's Circles

We often describe good presenters as having presence when they communicate. Sometimes that term is extended to leadership or executive presence, but what exactly is it? More importantly, do I have it?

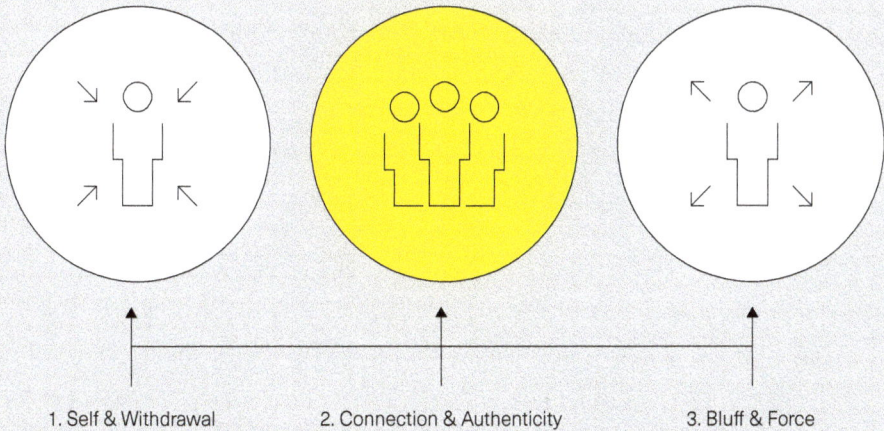

Figure 3: Rodenburg's Three Circles of Energy

1. Self & Withdrawal   2. Connection & Authenticity   3. Bluff & Force

Like an actor stepping on stage, delivering a presentation places us under pressure. Rodenburg observed that pressure manifests through performers' bodies as three types of energy movements. She calls them the first, second and third circles.

The first circle is the energy of self and withdrawal. This is inward-moving, drawing energy toward the self. Think of a timid, mumbling presenter, who speaks very quietly, is unsteady on their feet, rarely makes eye contact and reads from their slides.

Let's skip over the second circle for the moment.

The third circle is the energy of bluff and force, and is the opposite of the first. It is generalised energy, forced outward. Think of the agitated, frenetic presenter who speaks too forcefully for the room, dominates, over gesticulates, and strides about randomly.

Between the first and third sits the second circle – the energy of connection and authenticity. Focussed and present, it is the energy of equality that travels like an invisible figure eight back and forth between you and your audience. Think of the wonderful presenter who compels you to listen without pressure or guilt. Or the speaker who makes you feel like you're having a terrifically engaging conversation. It is powerful, authentic energy, free from force or submissiveness.

At the heart of Rodenburg's circles sits the deep human need for connection. To relate to our audience, we need to be present *with* them, not just present *to* them. If not, the connection becomes very difficult. That's why great speakers, in their own way, always strive to be in the second circle. Their energy signals clearly, 'I am here, and this is me.' They are powerful, and rather than dominate or drain our power, they ignite it.

Right, let's get into the archetypes.

The Archetypes of Organisational Speakers

As you track from left to right in the model, you'll see there are three states of energy, moving from *Under-energised* into *Authenticity & Connection* and on to *Over-energised*. Notice the influence of Rodenburg's Circles here? There's also a transition up the left side, from *In the Shadows* through the *Twilight Zone* and into *In the Spotlight*.

The spotlight metaphor is at the heart of this book. To be *In the Spotlight* means presenting with impact. If you're in *The Twilight Zone* or *In the Shadows,* your full potential is not yet realised.

Let's take a moment here. Which archetype do you default to when you're at your worst? What about when you're at your best? Or when you're winging it? With a high-status audience? Or when you're

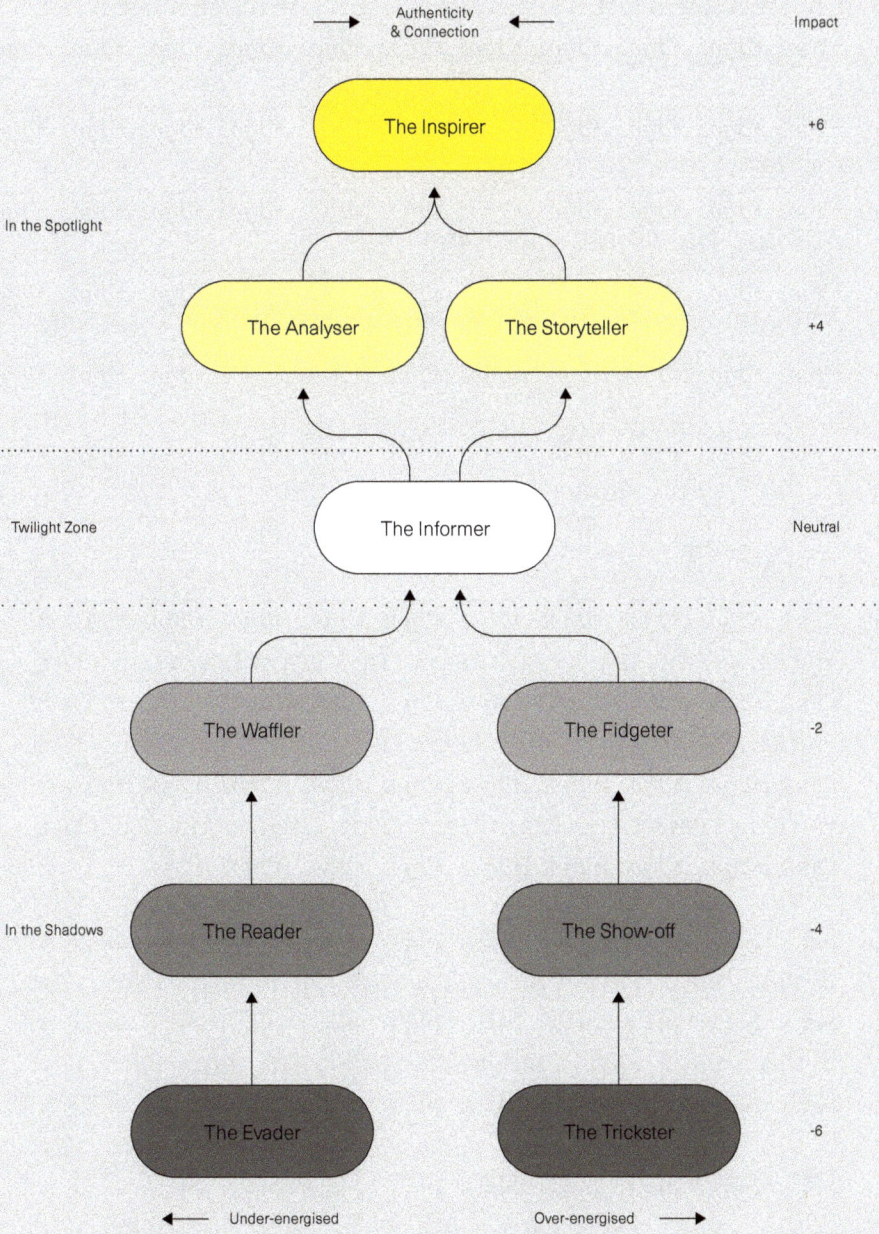

Figure 4: The archetypes of organisational speakers

coasting? What's the best you've ever been? You might discover that your primary archetype changes depending on the circumstance or the audience. In fact, you'll likely relate to a couple.

If you see yourself consistently in the shadows, sincerely ask yourself, 'Why am I here?'

Beware the shadow keepers

Three things will keep you trapped in the shadows as a presenter. I call these your shadow keepers. They are:

1. Insufficient subject knowledge

2. Poor preparation

3. Self-limiting beliefs

Their collective effect is like bumping into your ex at the supermarket. Your anxiety ramps up, which pulls you out of presence into an *under-energised* or *over-energised* state: '*I'm gonna pretend I didn't see them and keep reading the back of this pickle jar*' or '*I'm gonna strut right up with my rebound bod and be maniacally friendly.*' Either way, you're not yourself. Getting these shadow keepers under control is the shortcut to your spotlight.

The first shadow keeper, insufficient subject knowledge, is your responsibility. It's over to you to ensure you know your stuff. The second, poor preparation, will be overcome by following the process in this book. The third, self-limiting beliefs, may take a little more time, but getting the first two under control will be a massive help.

Let's not get too obsessed

A quick reminder to keep perspective. As the statistician George Box noted, 'All models are flawed, but some are useful.' These archetypes draw attention to typical patterns of behaviour and their impact on your audience. They are not representative of how competent you are at your job or the value you bring in other areas of your life. They are simply patterns from which you may examine and adjust your communication habits – both good and bad. Improvement and growth are the goals here.

What if you made a commitment to yourself, right now, to always be in the spotlight? Go on. Why not? If you follow the process introduced later in this book, it's entirely possible. What if your entire team committed? Or better yet, your entire company! What if you never had to sit through a bad presentation again? Imagine that!

The Shadow Archetypes

There are six Shadow Archetypes (the bottom half of the model). The Evader, The Reader and The Waffler will typically present in an under-energised (first circle) state, while The Trickster, The Show-off and The Fidgeter are typically over-energised (third circle).

Each archetype has specific behavioural traits, as we'll discuss below. For example, the Reader may turn from their audience to read their slides, while the Fidgeter might pace agitatedly around the room. Understanding these traits helps us recognise them in ourselves and replace them with more effective presenting habits.

Displaying too many of these shadow traits means audiences will struggle to connect with your ideas, and the impact of your presentation will be lessened. You may have difficulty being noticed or heard. At worst, your audience may lose trust in your abilities. Don't worry. We've all been there at some point. Nevertheless, if you are the presenter and we are your audience, it is your responsibility not to bore, confuse, manipulate, or waste our time. And if you are demonstrating these traits, then that's exactly what you risk doing.

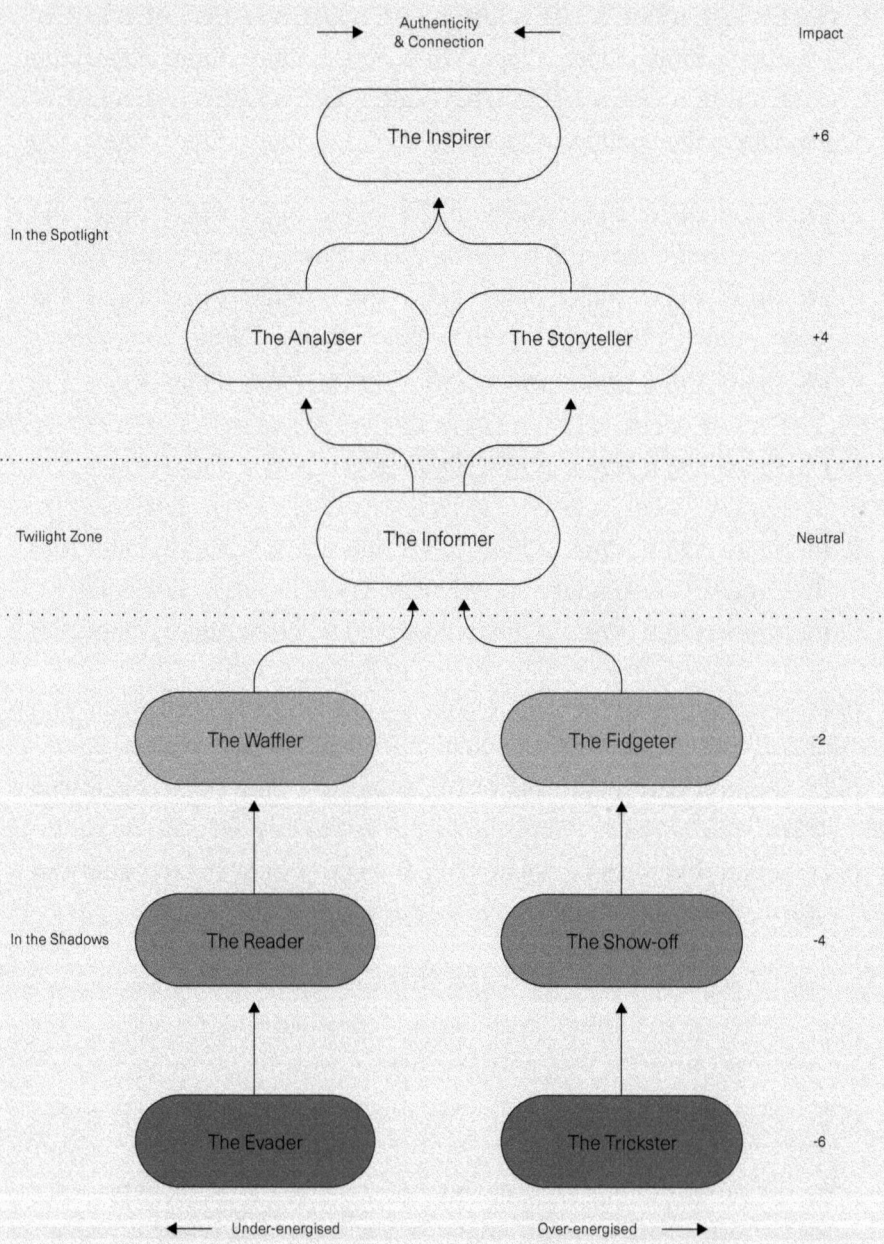

Figure 5: The Shadow Archetypes

The first three archetypes we'll examine are those at the bottom left of the model. These I classify as under-energised (first circle) and in the shadows.

The Evader

Chief shadow keeper: Self-limiting beliefs

State: Fearful

Impression: Invisible

Audience impact: Powerless

If the thought of presenting is terrifying, and you'll go to almost any length to avoid it, then The Evader is your dominant archetype. You're not alone in your evasion. By some estimates, up to seventy-five per cent of the adult population have some form of glossophobia (the technical name for fear of public speaking).[2]

Generally, The Evader is trapped in a cycle of avoidance. I call this [*lowers voice*] the shadow vortex. Think of it as a self-fulfilling prophecy with a twist of self-sabotage. It all starts with a strong narrative you repeat over and over (you might even be unaware that you do it). It goes something like, 'I'm terrified of presenting,' 'I hate this so much,' 'I just don't have the gift of the gab,' or 'Presenting is so not my thing.' The trouble is that this narrative starves you of opportunities to gain experience. See where I'm heading?

When you can no longer avoid presenting, you'll freak out because you lack the safety of a good process, and you've yet to experience the feeling of success that a good process will bring. But here's the real stickler. You get up there, you do it, and guess what? You really do suck. No two ways about it. You know it, and despite a few patronising nods of encouragement, your audience does too. The whole time you feel like Cersei Lannister on her *Game of Thrones'* walk of shame. You're exhausted, you've had no sleep, and you're an emotional wreck. After an eternity, the presentation's finally over and the only tangible outcome? The reinforcement of the narrative that *You. Don't. Belong. Up. There.* And so the cycle continues...

Until, of course, you decide to change the story.

The Reader

Chief shadow keeper: Insufficient Subject Knowledge

State: Nervous

Impression: Uncertain

Audience impact: Boring

If your idea of delivering a presentation is to diligently read your slides or notes, then, dear reader, you are The Reader. Think about this for a moment. If all you're doing is reading your slides, why not let your audience do it for themselves? What is the point of being there?

I know you'll have your reasons for reading. Perhaps you're unfamiliar with your content, or you're worried you'll veer off track and mind-blank on something important. Maybe your anxiety is such that you feel reading is the only way you'll make it through. I get it – but here's the brutal truth. It's boring. If all your energy is directed into your notes or at the screen, then we miss out on connecting with you. It's that connection that keeps us interested. And the consequence? Audiences perceive The Reader as being under-prepared, uncertain or afraid. And very quickly, the presentation feels tedious for all concerned.

Another common trait that manifests across many shadow archetypes, but particularly in The Reader, is the tendency to begin presentations with an apology. 'Sorry, I haven't had a chance to look through these slides yet,' 'Sorry, I'm really terrible at presenting,' or 'Sorry, I know these slides are really complicated but...,' Yawn. I'm bored even writing about them. And they're not even apologies, are they? They're excuses.

Reading is appropriate in some communication scenarios, but they're more likely to be a formal statement or prepared speech than a presentation. If you're the Governor of the Reserve Bank announcing a dramatic hike in the official cash rate, I get the importance of reading a prepared statement from notes or a teleprompter. In some high-stakes scenarios, the need for absolute precision will trump everything else.

For presentations, however, avoid reading. Now before you get any ideas, I'm certainly not recommending that you memorise your entire presentation. That would take far too much time. Rather, try talking freely to a well-planned series of points. More on that later.

The Waffler

Chief shadow keeper: Poor preparation

State: Oblivious

Impression: Indulgent

Audience impact: Frustrating

If you find yourself talking around in circles and struggling to get to the point, then chances are your dominant archetype is The Waffler. I've encountered two types of wafflers: the self-conscious and the self-indulgent.

The self-conscious waffler knows their tendency all too well, but they still work themselves in circles – much to their frustration. The self-indulgent waffler rambles on and on and on. Despite clear audience signals of restlessness or impatience, they remain blissfully oblivious and carry-on waffling. They may also head off on frustrating tangents, be easily distracted and randomly pontificate on irrelevant points.

In fact, it's entirely possible to leave The Waffler's presentation no wiser than when you entered. Consequently, audiences can think The Waffler is disrespectful of their time, frustrating and, at worst, agonising to listen to. Further Waffler traits include excessive corporate jargon, repetitive word use, hedging statements: 'I guess what I wanted to talk about...' or 'It's sort of like...' and visual aids that don't align with what they're saying.

Now let's examine the archetypes that appear on the bottom right of the model. These I classify as over-energised (third circle) and in the shadows.

The Trickster

Chief shadow keeper: Insufficient subject knowledge

State: Bluff

Impression: Arrogant

Audience impact: Divisive

Traits of The Trickster generally manifest in presenters who, at their core, have a deep fear of being found out or found wanting. This fear can manifest from being under-experienced or ill-equipped for their job, out of their depth with the subject matter, feeling a deep sense of cultural or organisational exclusion or not believing what they're presenting to be right or true.

The most common trait is hyper-communicating, where fast-paced sentences bleed into each other with no breaks or pauses, and similar points and phrases are repeated unnecessarily. These sentences are often said with great conviction and laced with buzz words and company jargon, but the meaning is obscure or incoherent.

Less common is The Trickster narcissist. This greasy character is highly adept at manipulation and deception, even straight-out intimidation. They can be confident and charming, but many see their energy as too slick or salesy. They are all sizzle and no sausage.

We frequently mistake their confidence for competence, which is why it is quite possible to find The Trickster narcissist in senior positions of leadership and influence. Interestingly, a recent meta-analysis of narcissistic leadership traits showed that their competence almost always falls below average for their peer group.[3] As such, this archetype's favourite audience is the ill-informed, the greedy or the vulnerable.

The Show-off

Chief shadow keeper: Poor preparation

State: Performative

Impression: Inauthentic

Audience impact: Irritating

If you make statements like: 'I just like to wing it,' or 'Practising just makes me worse,' then your dominant archetype could be The Show-off. They are the organisation's performers – often entertaining but prone to a lack of substance or attention to detail. They love an audience but can be lazy in their preparation and tend to rely on their confidence and likability to wing it. Consequently, they risk missing the mark and being superficial in their argument. When caught on the hop, The Show-off is quick to dazzle with humour, random stories, or complex language to detract from a lack of preparation or a lack of clarity.

The physicality of The Show-off can feel over-exuberant with gestures that seem too big rather than natural and a vocal tone too contrived rather than conversational. They easily get carried away with their presentation, wishing to impress with their delivery and flair. The cumulative effect for their audience is a feeling of being talked *at* rather than talked *to*. They are good for the stage, but in an organisational context, they can seem inauthentic – especially with introverts, high-status or expert audiences and others who prefer authenticity over theatricality. As such, The Show-off risks developing a show-pony or grandstanding reputation. 'All style and no substance' or 'all talk and no action.' When this archetype takes the time to prepare consistently and diligently, they can quickly move into their Spotlight and become exceptional presenters.

The Fidgeter

Chief shadow keeper: Self-limiting beliefs

State: Self-conscious

Impression: Anxious

Audience impact: Distracting

If you find it difficult to stand still when presenting, your dominant archetype could be The Fidgeter. Fidgeters manifest distracting physical and vocal habits – most of which they're entirely oblivious to. These could be pacing, rocking or swaying, hand wringing, playing with objects like pens, keys in pockets or jewellery and skimming, sporadic eye contact. Vocally, they may have lots of filled pauses (ums and ahs) and a tendency to up-glide at the end of sentences. Together these habits create an impression of self-consciousness and agitation. It's not uncommon for some audience members to become fixated on The Fidgeter's idiosyncrasies and completely distracted from the core message.

As with many of the earlier archetypes, if you relate to The Fidgeter, you struggle to be comfortable when all eyes are on you. However, here's the frustrating paradox. Your vocal and physical restlessness ends up drawing more attention to yourself. Dammit!

Generally, these excess movements are simply physical manifestations of your nerves and anxiety. Becoming conscious of their effect on your body and voice is the start of keeping them in check. After all, it's unlikely these habits will appear when you're relaxed in everyday conversation. Consider what message your body language and vocal quirks are sending to your audience. Are they enhancing or detracting from your presentation?

The Twilight Zone

This is the threshold between the shadows and the spotlight, and here sits the most common type of organisational communicator, the Informer. Many of you may be trapped here, struggling to transition to greater impact. Some may find this a comfortable place and be fearful of or indifferent to progressing further. Or perhaps you feel you simply do not have the innate abilities to progress – which, of course, is a myth.

The Informer

Primary shadow keeper: Any three

State: Flat

Impression: Forgettable

Audience impact: Neutral

Of the thousands of presentations I've seen over the years, The Informer is, by far, the most represented archetype. If you've taught yourself to muddle through your presentations without too much drama, and they're not awful, but not particularly great either, chances are you're an Informer.

I sometimes get asked about the single biggest issue I see when coaching presenters. My answer has nothing to do with delivery

Authenticity
& Connection

Impact

→   ←

The Inspirer

+6

In the Spotlight

The Analyser   The Storyteller

+4

Twilight Zone

The Informer

Neutral

The Waffler   The Fidgeter

-2

In the Shadows   The Reader   The Show-off

-4

The Evader   The Trickster

-6

← Under-energised   Over-energised →

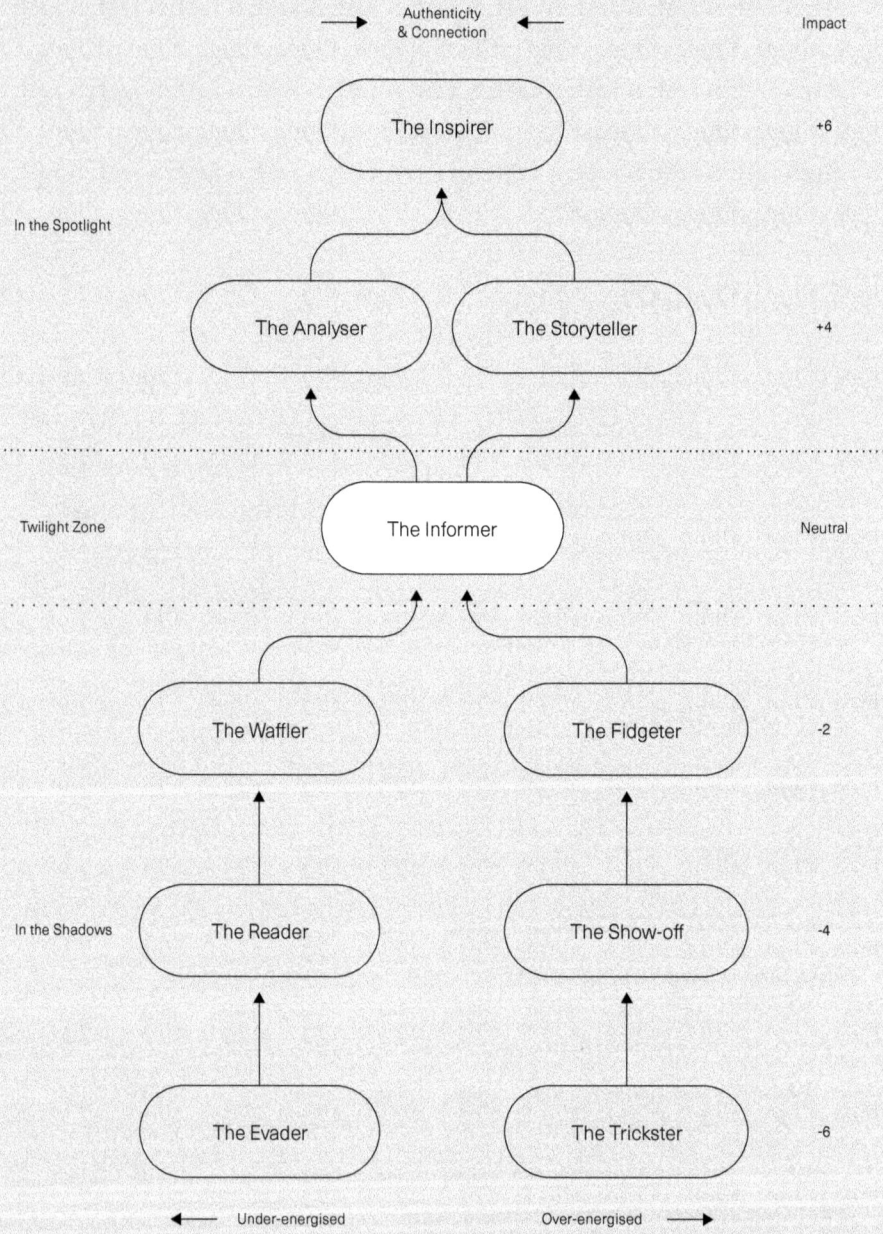

Figure 6: The Twilight Zone

skills. I think the biggest problem is information without intention – where the presenter hasn't truly defined why they're presenting so their content lacks purpose and fails to inspire action. That means the moment the audience leaves, it's a mostly forgotten experience – lost in the great organisation gyre of pointless presentations. The chief suspect in the crime of pointless presentations? The Informer – the presentation equivalent of the battery hen.

Let me put it another way. Imagine you're required to attend a presentation, and you ask the presenter: 'Hey Gurv, what's the presentation about tomorrow?' And Gurv's response is: 'Ummm, well...I'm just gonna talk through some stuff, some of it might be relevant to you, but honestly, most of it probably won't be. Oh, and the relevant stuff? You'll have to work that out for yourself. But don't worry, it'll be in there somewhere.' Gurv is the classic Informer.

As The Informer, your default presentation is likely the report or the update – and you'll do plenty of them. In fact, you're likely to have progressed from one of the six shadow archetypes purely through years of having to present. You may have already learnt to manage many of the visual and aural signs of agitation or anxiety, but because The Informer's presentations often lack clear intention, your delivery style tends to mirror that lack. It's best described as being a bit flat. You may be hesitant to drive action, have a strong point of view, or generate emotion in your audience. There's a colourlessness or austerity to your communication style, which audiences can mistake for indifference or disengagement.

Of course, that assessment could be entirely accurate as you may well be bored, disengaged, burnt out, under-stimulated or poorly managed. You may have repeatedly tried to speak up, share ideas and affect change, only to be ignored, pushed back, or silenced. Perhaps a defeatist attitude has set in. That can be prevalent in organisations or teams that have gone through prolonged disruption. At worst, you might believe your ideas no longer matter, that you can't make a difference, or it's not worth the hassle to try. That's why The Informer archetype sits in the Twilight Zone of this model. Twilight happens at dawn and dusk, and while usually a transition point, it can symbolise the beginning or the end of a presentation skills journey.

What will it be for you?

In the Spotlight

Being 'In the Spotlight' means you consistently realise your potential as a presenter, through a process of continual improvement. The spotlight does not represent an end point; it grows and changes as your experience and career grows and changes. You just keep getting better.

There are three spotlight archetypes: The Analyser, The Storyteller and The Inspirer. When you are in the spotlight, your presentations are persuasive and powerful, and research suggests that you are more likely to be promoted, have engaged teams, and be paid more.[4] Audiences receive value from listening to what you have to say.

Add these archetypes to a reputation for competence, recognised status and humility, and your influence is further amplified. You will be sought-after for your expertise, knowledge and leadership. It is also highly likely that you will have a strong growth mindset and seek out opportunities to consistently work on your communication skills.

Authenticity → & Connection ← Impact

In the Spotlight

The Inspirer +6

The Analyser   The Storyteller +4

Twilight Zone

The Informer Neutral

The Waffler   The Fidgeter -2

In the Shadows

The Reader   The Show-off -4

The Evader   The Trickster -6

← Under-energised   Over-energised →

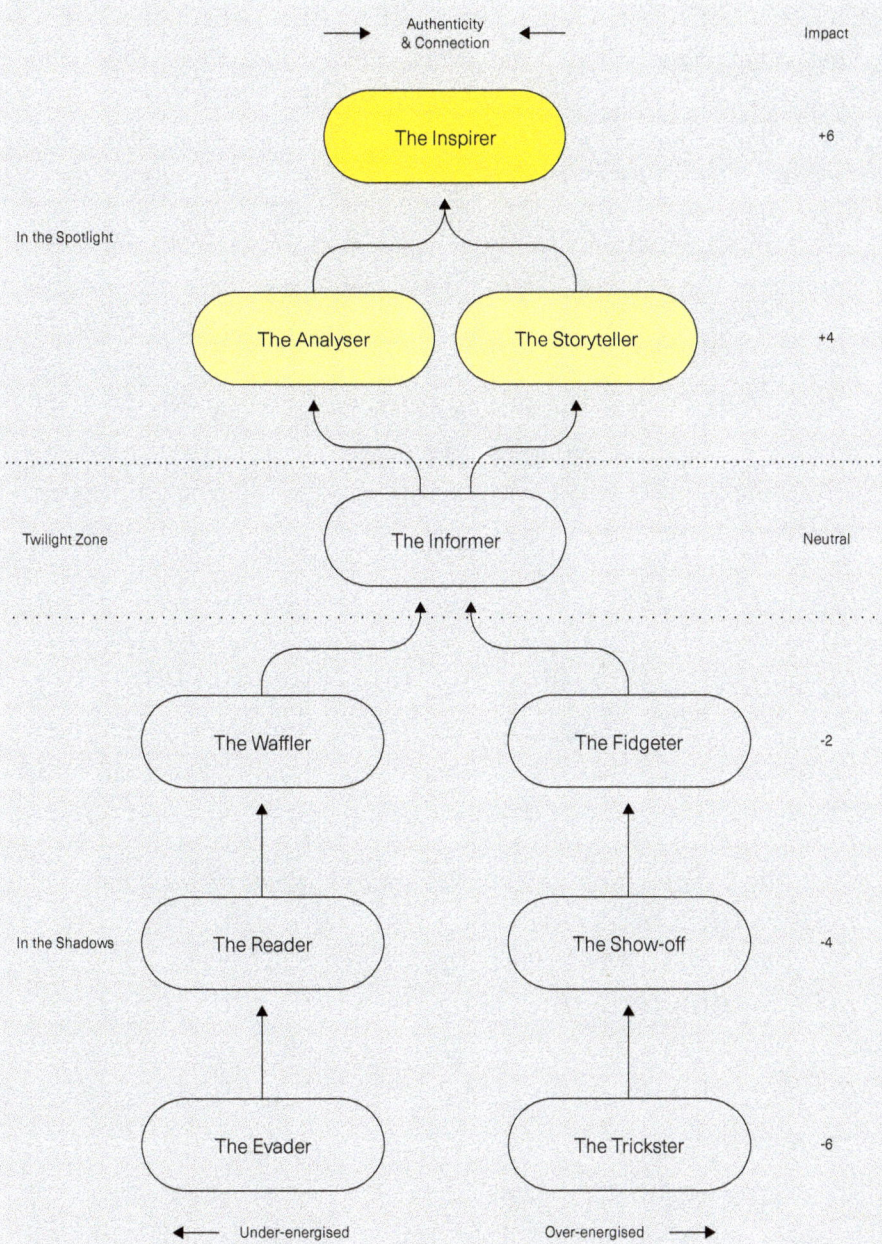

Figure 7: In the Spotlight

The Analyser

State: Confident

Impression: Competent

Audience impact: Persuasive

If you're The Analyser, you are adept at drawing insight from data, numbers and analytics, then clearly communicating that insight to drive better organisational decision-making. Your superpower is making the complicated simple. You can find patterns of meaning in disparate data sets and quickly aggregate noise into clear decision points. Even though you're likely technically or financially oriented, you understand that not everybody processes information the way you do and can appropriately tailor your messages to any audience.

You are comfortable in the spotlight, but you've likely worked hard at it over the years. You understand your persuasive strength lies not in colourful oratory or theatricality but in your ability to distil and synthesise information and share relevant and valuable insights. You will likely have a centred, grounded physicality, precision with language, a relaxed vocal presence, genuine tone and open outlook.

To further your impact, work on bringing elements of the Storyteller archetype into your presentations.

The Storyteller

State: Compelling

Impression: Authentic

Audience impact: Motivating

The Storyteller is comfortable wielding the most powerful tool in the presentation toolkit – the story. Where The Analyser is adept at linking with our minds, The Storyteller connects with our hearts.

They don't replace evidence, argument or ideas with stories; instead, use stories to reinforce and build on them. They understand the difference between stories and narratives, and their presentations are always engaging. They connect to us emotionally and may genuinely move us. Their language is creative but appropriate, making regular use of metaphor, analogy and other forms of figurative language. The Storyteller is physically animated but authentic, with a dynamic and engaging vocal presence.

To further your impact, work on bringing elements of The Analyser archetype into your presentations.

The Inspirer

State: Humble

Impression: Courageous

Audience impact: Powerful

The Inspirer is born when The Analyser and The Storyteller combine. Their magic is being a powerful, but rarely forceful, presenter. When they speak, people listen. They are proficient in all the tools of persuasion and deeply guided by their values. The Inspirer projects compassion, curiosity and kindness, but also strength, determination and focus. Every presentation is approached with courage and always diligently prepared. Their ideas are igniting and easy to follow. They are adept at adjusting their message to any audience while not sacrificing authenticity or succumbing to spin. If you're The Inspirer, you know where you fit, who you are and how you're of value.

Status and job title does not predict the Inspirer; they are across all areas of an organisation. What sets them apart is their consistent and glorious ability to say the right words in the right way at the right time. Like all the archetypes, their title is earned, not claimed. It is gifted from the hearts and minds of all those they inspire.

Beware the safety of the shadows

While archetypes operating in their spotlight are consistently successful at presenting, they are not always perfect. They will have yin to their yang – a shadow to their light. This can manifest when they have not prepared as well as they should have, when they've made incorrect assumptions about their audience, or when hubris has made them complacent.

In these situations, they can retreat to the shadows – the Analyser can fall back to The Waffler – the Storyteller back to The Show-off – even The Inspirer can be seen as The Trickster if their audience has lost trust and faith in them. Each archetype you embody at your best has a shadow you retreat to at your worst. The three shadow keepers are always ready to trap the ill-prepared.

Chapter Three

Getting the Brief

So, you've been asked to deliver a presentation.

Maybe your manager has requested that you present a financial update to the leadership team, or a conference organiser wants you to speak at their upcoming event. Perhaps you'll be delivering a stock-standard presentation that happens at every quarterly management meeting, or you've been asked to speak at a new employee induction on behalf of the HR team...tomorrow! Whatever the scenario, do not underestimate the power of a tight brief – and I'm not talking undies.

Loose briefs cause grief

If the presentation brief is not clear, your first job should be to politely seek further clarification from the requester as to why you've been asked and what outcome they want. Remember the number one issue of The Informer archetype? Information without intention.

I often see people delivering presentations without fully knowing why they were asked. When questioned, common responses are: 'Because we've just always done it this way,' or 'Because my boss asked me not to.' Yes, but *why* has your boss asked? Do you know their reasoning?

Here's an example. Say you're the Head of Digital at your company, and your boss, the GM of Marketing, has asked you to deliver a digital marketing update for the leadership team. He sent the following email at 5.30pm asking you to come to the senior leadership team (SLT) meeting. Tomorrow!

Hey there,

Adrienne [the CEO] has asked if you'd come along to the SLT tomorrow and give a quick update to the team on where we're at with digital? Sorry for the short notice. Should be relatively straight forward so don't stress about it.

Thanks heaps,

Andy

I'm sure, dear reader, you've received something similar in the past – am I right? Or worse, are you guilty of sending this? Now is an excellent time to change your ways.

Ok, let's break down the issues. First, there's zero time to prepare, so you're caught on the hop. Will you stay up all night preparing the wrong presentation?

Next, there's no indication of purpose. Why have they asked you to present? What's the background context? What do they want you to cover? What questions do they want to be answered, or what reassurances given? The list can go on and on.

The timing boundaries are unclear. How long do you have to present? Is it five minutes, ten, twenty? A fifteen-minute presentation is vastly different to a five-minute stand-up. What about questions? Is there time allotted for those? What time of day will you be presenting to them? First thing in the morning when they're fresh and energised, or late in the day when they're fatigued after sitting through two hours of waffling Tony from Health and Safety?

Next. The location. There's no mention of where you'll be presenting, so you guess it'll be the boardroom. But that has its own challenges. The screen is at the front of the room, but the HDMI cable you need to plug into is at the back, meaning you either must stand at the back of the room to advance your slides [avoid this], ask someone to advance them for you [avoid this even more], or remember to take your remote clicker [good idea]. What's more, you're not even sure they want a slide deck.

So yes, loose briefs do indeed cause grief. They increase your risk of being ambushed by an alpha ego, being irrelevant, waffling on too long, or looking out of your depth. Make sure you ask questions of the requester – and get the answers in writing if you can. That way, if you are ambushed with questions you're not prepared for, at least you've got a good excuse.

Here's what Andy's email should have said:

Evening,

Adrienne wanted you to come along to the SLT meeting tomorrow to give a quick update on where we're at with digital. I've asked if we can push it out until next week's meeting to give you more time to prepare. She's happy with that. Essentially, a few of the SLT are a little concerned about the push-back we're getting from store owners as we funnel our traditional print and radio budgets into more digital channels. They're on board with the strategy, but they want to be better equipped to explain the why and have that conversation with their store managers. As you know, there's a ton of technical jargon involved, but my suggestion is to keep it simple and high-level for them. Give some attention to the top three benefits our new focus on digital channels is bringing to our overall strategy – make sure you share some of the great data we're seeing – Adrienne loves to get into the numbers.

They've given us 30 mins next Wednesday and want you first up. I'll do a quick intro, then hand over to you. Expect to be peppered with questions as you go, so keep the actual presentation about 15 mins total with time for questions during or after. I'll be there to back you up if you get any curveballs.

The full SLT will be present, plus a couple of board members, so it's a good chance for you to build your credibility with them and share some of the amazing work you've been doing. And remember, they loathe complicated slide decks, so keep your visuals super simple and to the point.

Sing out if you have any more questions. I'm free for a quick run-through on the Tuesday arvo if that suits?

Cheers,

Andy

Much better, thank you Andy.

To reiterate. If the brief you've been given is loose, be proactive and seek clarification immediately. Know your playing field.

Wait, know your playing field?

I promise this will be my only sporting metaphor. Just as weather and turf conditions can have a major effect on the outcome of a sporting match, so too your environment can affect the outcome of your presentation. Any great sporting team will work to understand the subtleties and idiosyncrasies of their playing field, and you too should understand and prepare for the environment in which you will present.

Just think of the number of presentations you've seen where the presenter has struggled to get their technology working properly, has booked a meeting room that's too small, or arrives to find the room is not correctly set up, or is late because they couldn't find a park, or can't get their microphone working, or doesn't have the correct dongle...you get the idea.

Within minutes the audience is bored and agitated. To mitigate these risks, consider your environment before you start preparing. You may not have all the details yet, and that's ok. Just start gathering all the information you can. I call this 'knowing your playing field' – the boundaries of timing, setting and equipment.

Timing is everything

Understanding timing gives important restrictions to your presentation structure. There are three aspects to consider. First, confirm the date – this will tell you how long you've got to prepare.

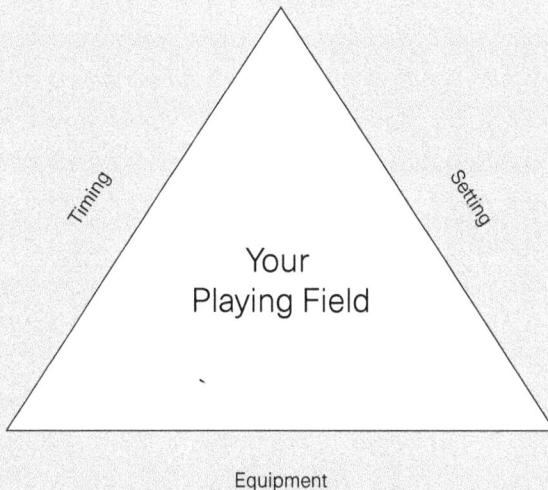

Figure 8: Define your playing field

Second, know how long you've got to deliver. And third, be aware of the time of day you'll be presenting.

If there's one thing everyone's short on, it's time. That's why it's critical to respect the time your audience is giving and don't take any more than you absolutely need. If a presenter has done their work well, few presentations need to last longer than thirty minutes. That's right, thirty minutes.

And that brings me to one of the most common presentation fails – the over-time presentation (I'm looking at you, Waffler). That is the presenter who gets twenty minutes into a thirty-minute time slot and suddenly realises they're only a quarter of the way through their slide deck. Cue frantic apologies and a flutter of slides, muttering, 'Look, I'll just skip over this next section as it's not that important.' If it's not essential, why is it in your presentation? Don't waste our time.

The main reasons people go over time are either overestimating the amount of content they can get through or underestimating their audience's level of engagement and interaction. Both are preventable with good planning.

Here's a good rule of thumb. When given your time slot, shave off about twenty per cent of your allowed time. For example, if you have thirty minutes, aim to finish in under twenty. And make sure you've checked expectations around questions. For example, a thirty-minute time slot might mean twenty minutes for the presentation with ten minutes at the end for questions.

Don't underestimate the impact of the time of day on your ability to connect. The fatigue level of your audience will help or hinder you. Usually, you won't have much choice in setting a start time, but choose wisely and strategically if you do. Generally, a morning slot earlier in the week is better than an afternoon later. Who wants to be sitting in a presentation at 4pm on Friday?

Timing questions to ask:

- What's the date of the presentation?
- How long do you have to prepare?
- How long do you have to present (always use less time)?
- What's the start time? Can you set this?
- If part of a conference, who's on before and after you?

Make the setting work

The setting is where your presentation will take place – either virtually or in person. It is important to differentiate between the two. A presentation that may work well in an in-person setting may not work as well virtually – and vice-versa. It's critical that your setting works to facilitate a good connection with your audience.

A few years back, I ran a series of one-day business presentation skills programmes in Wellington for a long-standing client. I arrived on the morning to set up but found our usual training room, a spacious setting with great technology and beautiful views over the harbour, had been commandeered by senior management for an important board meeting. Alas, we'd been relocated to the only other room available that day – the Fishbowl – a pokey little meeting room in the centre of the main office floor partitioned off with glass walls.

The Fishbowl was designed to seat about six comfortably for spontaneous meetings, not nine people for an entire day. It lacked privacy, and the air-conditioning was poor, so it was hot and stuffy. There was no natural light, and it was cramped and uncomfortable. I could tell the participants were immediately self-conscious about being visible to their colleagues.

Unfortunately, we had to make it work. It was a very challenging day for all involved. Engagement and energy levels plummeted as people felt inhibited and self-conscious. Concentration levels lapsed. People grew restless, and in the afternoon, they were visibly exhausted.

All you can do in such situations is push on as best you can and allow plenty of breaks. However, I was well and truly off my game. As expected, the post-programme feedback survey was average. When briefing programme organisers, I now make it very clear that the training room needs to be fit for purpose and not subject to executive usurpers.

But no matter how well prepared, it's inevitable that at some point you'll have to present in environments that are less than ideal. All you can do is suck it up as best you can. I have a good deal of sympathy for anyone who must adapt unexpectedly to a setting that actively hinders their ability to connect. But I have little sympathy for presenters who find themselves in crappy environments through poor planning on their part. Do not underestimate how much the wrong setting can throw you, so be sure to choose an appropriate space to deliver your message.

A word on virtual settings

Virtual environments present their own unique challenges. Usually, these revolve around maintaining engagement and minimising an audience's external distractions. After all, it's far easier for the audience to check out of your virtual presentation and start scrolling through their Instagram feed than it is in-person.

Furthermore, not all virtual platforms are created equal. Some have far better tools for interaction than others. At the time of writing, Zoom is still outperforming its competitors regarding user-friendliness, engagement tools and broadcast reliability.

Timing is even more critical when presenting virtually. For example, when we began delivering our two-day business presentation skills workshop online, we had to rethink the delivery format completely. Nobody wants to be on Zoom for two full days in a row. That would be punishing.

What did we do instead? We started by splitting our usual group of eight participants into two groups of four. This allowed for much better interaction without the awkwardness and lag of talking on Zoom in large groups. We experimented with different timings but eventually agreed that three two-hour sessions over three days for each group of four worked best for both audience and presenter. It's a further example of how the choice of the environment affects the format of the presentation. That is why it's essential to consider these right at the beginning.

Setting questions to ask:

- Is the presentation virtual or in-person?
- If virtual, what is the communication platform (e.g. Zoom, Google Meet, Microsoft Teams)
- What is the presenting location?
- If offsite, what's the travel time and is parking available?
- How many people will be in the audience?
- What's the seating and visual aid layout?
- What's the dress code?
- Who will introduce you?
- Can you get access before setup or rehearse?

Choose the right equipment

Equipment represents the technology and tools you use during your presentation. If you're presenting in-person, the most common include a data projector or flatscreen television, microphone, whiteboard, flip charts, a comfort monitor to prompt your next slides, your computer, and a clicker or slide advancer.

When presenting in new environments, it is particularly important to understand what equipment is available (and their limitations).

Let's say you're a graphic designer, and you've prepared a new brand launch presentation to deliver onsite for your client, a medium-sized construction firm. You've got a room full of managers eager and excited to see the new reveal. To your horror, you discover their antiquated, internal AV system has not had a firmware update since installation and has major issues running HDMI streams from newer Macs. 'Oh you're running a Mac? Yeah, we've been having trouble with Macs lately.'

You spend a frantic fifteen minutes trying to get your technology to sync, but it fails. You end up emailing the presentation to the client only to discover their mail server rejects it because the file size is too large. So you decide to copy your presentation to a memory stick and run it off the client's computer. By this time, you've running fifteen minutes late, and your nerves are through the roof and the impact of your brand reveal is considerably compromised. A far-fetched example you say? Not at all. A participant recounted this story to me in a recent programme.

Equipment failure remains one of the most common derailers of presentations. Murphy's Law always applies – if it can go wrong, it likely will. Your job is to try to mitigate all unexpected situations as best you can. Sure, there's always going to be something that you can never prepare for, but you'll be amazed at how a few simple questions in advance can reduce the risk of derailing your presentation.

Equipment questions to ask

- What equipment will you need and what will be provided? AV equipment, whiteboard, flipcharts, lectern?

- Will you need a microphone? If so, will it be lapel, handheld or podium?

- Which visual medium will be most appropriate?

- Will there be a location technician/IT person available?

- Where will you have an accessible back-up of your presentation?

By now, you'll begin to see it's almost impossible to construct a great presentation without first understanding your playing field – the essential boundaries of time, setting and equipment. Understanding them well means you can use them to your advantage.

Beware organisational artifacts

If ever a phrase makes me want to roll my eyes, it's, 'That's the way we've always done it.' Often it's associated with reporting or updating style presentations. These presentations are likely highly templated – and usually for a good reason. If you're delivering a KPI update every month, you don't need to build a new presentation from scratch every time. It makes sense to simplify the process with a templated presentation and adjust the figures each month.

However, the likely issue is that template was created by Greg from sales back in 2011. At that time, it was great. Nice and simple, fit for purpose, clear on outcomes, and a great addendum to Greg, a capable communicator. But you're the fourth person in the role since Greg

2011, and every person since has added a few more slides. The slide deck is now a cluttered mess.

What's more, the sales strategy has changed since Greg's day, and some of the KPIs are no longer relevant. Nobody who has inherited the presentation has bothered to ask if it's still fit for purpose. It's become a stale organisational artefact, delivered without question. Seventy-five per cent of the presentation is never touched, as the presenter has become adept at skipping through to get to the relevant bits. Everyone becomes complicit in the way it has always been done. You've all been hypnotised. Snap out of it.

If you're relating to this, then now's the perfect opportunity to change it up. I know what you're thinking. Is it worth it? Can I be bothered? It's too much work. And yes, change will often meet resistance. If your new presentation is done right and communicates clear value and actionable insight, your audience will thank you for it. It's a terrific way to build your credibility and reputation as a good communicator, and a pro-active and valuable team member.

Right then. Now that we're clear on the brief, let's crack into creating the presentation.

Chapter Quick Tips: *Getting the Brief*

- Get clear on the brief – including *why* you've been asked to present, what's to be covered and outcomes needed.

- Understand your playing field – the boundaries of timing, setting and equipment.

- Timing: When will the presentation be? How much time do you have to present? What time of day will you present?

- Setting: Will the presentation be virtual or in-person? What platform or what location? How will the room be arranged?

- Equipment: What equipment will you need and what will be provided? AV equipment, whiteboard, flipcharts, lectern, mic?

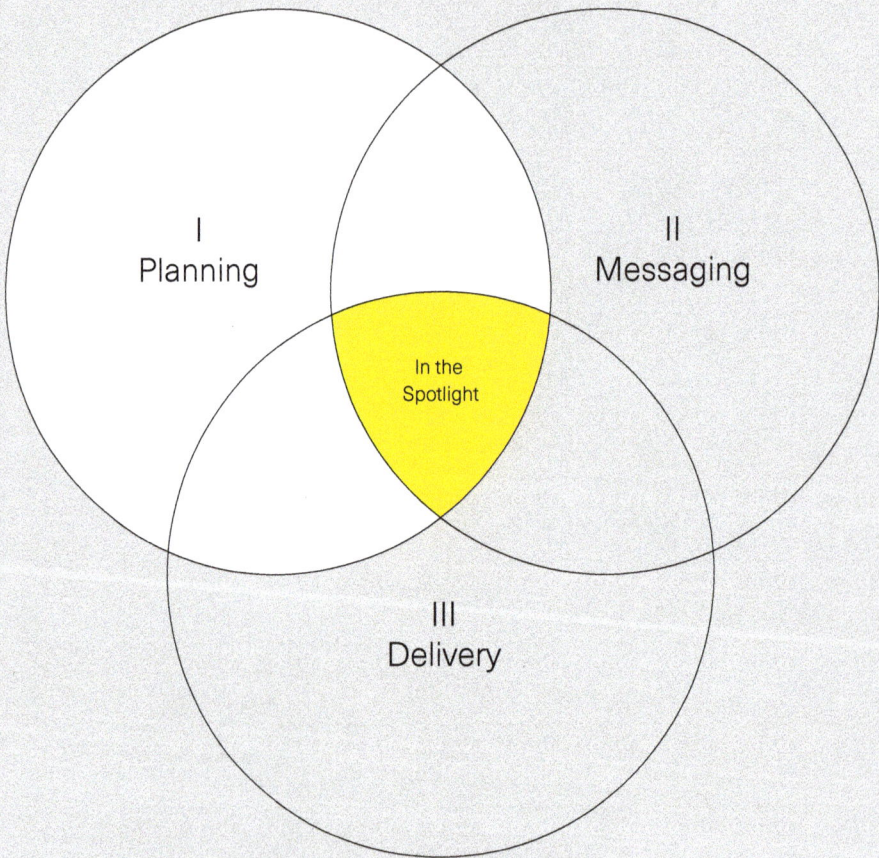

Section I
Planning

Chapter Four

The Audience – Point A

It might surprise you to hear that the most important element in any presentation is your audience. After all, your presentation is for *them*, not for you. The only reason you are presenting is to connect your ideas to them in a way that elicits some form of action. The deeper you understand them, the better your chances at doing that. In her book, *Persuasive Presentations,* presentation guru Nancy Duarte includes a terrific quote from AT&T executive Ken Haemer: 'Designing a presentation without an audience in mind is like writing a love letter and addressing it 'to whom it may concern.'[1]

Respect your audience

Respecting your audience means considering their needs and designing your message for them. Think for a moment about everything you loathe about bad business presentations; running over time, presenters that can't be heard or understood, monotonous droning, irrelevant content, slides that are overcomplicated and impossible to comprehend, presenters reading rather than connecting with you. These issues fail to place the audience's needs as the priority, and essentially, they are disrespectful. Once you develop your presentations through a frame of respect, everything changes.

A harsh lesson

Author Stephen Covey wrote that empathy is at the core of great communication. First, we must seek to understand, then to be understood.[2] Misunderstanding or making incorrect assumptions about your audience can be perilous. I learned this the hard way.

About a year into running my consultancy, I picked up a major multi-national tech company as a client. I was thrilled, as this was a big deal for my fledgling business. I was asked to deliver an afternoon session on Presentation Skills and PowerPoint to a group of eight middle managers in their Auckland office. If it went well, we'd schedule another. No problem. I met with the GM of HR, Sandy, and she gave me a great brief on the audience. I did my prep, delivered the programme, and it went so well that HR booked me immediately for the second group a few weeks later. I delivered again. That too went well. Everyone was happy.

A couple of weeks later, I got a rather panicked Monday afternoon phone call from Kate, Sandy's executive assistant. She asked if I did any sessions on business storytelling. Sandy was currently facilitating a week-long workshop with a group of managers, and the trainer she'd arranged for Wednesday had to pull out at the last minute. Was I available to come in and run a morning workshop?

At the time, business storytelling was just starting to become the 'skill du jour' in corporate land, so I immediately saw it as a great chance to test some ideas. I'd been delivering a weekend workshop on solo performance and storytelling for Community Education at the University of Auckland but hadn't yet run it as a specific programme for corporates. No problem, I thought, I could adapt my material and apply it to this. 'Yes, I can deliver that. How many people in the room?' 'I think about twenty-five,' she replied quickly.

Kate seemed busy, so I ended the call with a quick confirmation of time. At this point, the largest workshop I'd facilitated was for about fifteen people, so my heart gave a little jump at twenty-five. I knew I had to get used to training bigger audiences. It can't be that different, right?

I had a little less than forty-eight hours, so quickly got to work and pulled together what I thought was an ok session. To be safe, I figured I'd print thirty handouts and worksheets. My previous sessions at the company had given me what I felt was an ok knowledge of the type of audience to expect. I was ready.

Or at least I thought I was.

I arrived at the client about 8.45 am to set up. I was due to start at 9.15 am. Kate met me at reception and took me through to their learning centre. 'They're just doing their morning reflection session,' she said enthusiastically, 'they're really engaged, but a few are still a bit jet-lagged.'

'Wait, what? Jet-lagged?'

'Yeah, most have come in from Hong Kong, and there's a couple from Shanghai and Manila.'

'Oh, right, of course. Ahhh, remind me again what this group calls themselves?' I asked casually.

'APET,' she replied, 'The Asia Pacific Excel Team.'

It turns out that APET is a two-year leadership development programme for this company's absolute star employees. We're talking the high potentials, the best, the brightest, singled out from all over the Asia-Pacific region because of their talent, intelligence, and leadership potential. Every six months, they spend a week onsite in a different regional hub, training, networking, getting 'developed.' And intimidating inexperienced and under-prepared corporate trainers.

As we slipped into the back of the room, it got worse. Clearly, there were more than thirty people, and a quick count revealed almost fifty. I didn't even have enough collateral to hand out for the exercises I had planned!

'I thought there were only supposed to be about twenty-five people,' I whispered to Kate.

'Oh yeah, sorry, some of the Auckland management team who did your last course wanted to come and join. Hope that's ok?'

You know that feeling where you just want to run? Just gap it out of there as fast as you can? Pretend your house is on fire or your grandmother's had a stroke, and you're terribly sorry, but you need to leave immediately? That was me. My stomach was dropped into my feet. The floor was swayed. Instantly I was sweating. And I almost ran. I really did.

'I can run off some more copies of stuff if you need me to,' Kate said helpfully, sensing my panic.

'Yes, please,' and I scrambled through my case for the worksheets.

I thought I was prepared, but I certainly wasn't prepared for *them*.

A few minutes into my session, they knew it.

When confronted with a poorly prepared or inexperienced presenter, most audiences may react with indifference, boredom, restlessness, frustration, and maybe even pity. But now and then, you'll get one or two people who will take it upon themselves to try to expose you.

This audience had one such person.

Having just completed designing his own business storytelling workshop for the Hong Kong office, he was armed and dangerous. And he made sure everybody knew it. He wasn't hostile, just a relentless stream of questions that I should have been able to respond to but couldn't. To which he would then offer his answer. Worse still, they were good questions and really good answers. He clearly knew more about the topic as it related to their business than I did.

As every minute passed, more and more of my credibility was destroyed. I could see Sandy at the back of the room whispering to her colleague. I started having mind blanks and trouble linking my thoughts. I was wearing a light grey suit, and two large sweat patches had begun to form under my arms. It was a train-wreck.

I managed to get through the forty-five minutes until morning tea. As the room emptied, Sandy wasted no time coming up to me.

'Russell, how do you think this is going?'

'Not good,' I replied.

'Ok, look...I think it's best we rethink the rest of this session.'

It was a relief to hear her say those words, but it was deeply humiliating.

'Yes, absolutely,' I said.

I followed her lead, and we re-worked the morning into breakout groups and discussions. She was a master facilitator, and once the audience was back, she quickly took control of the room. She made it seem this was what we had planned for them all along – which I really appreciated. I floated from group to group, pretending to be involved but without the confidence to offer anything insightful. After they broke for lunch, I quickly packed my gear and quietly left. I never worked for that client again.

This experience remains the most humiliating I've had as a trainer. Thinking about it still makes me squirm. I was angry for not following my own advice. How could I put myself in a situation where I clearly should have known better? Then the blame: Why didn't Kate and Sandy give me a proper brief? I was doing them a favour! Why didn't Kate tell me the Auckland managers would also be joining?

It was a brutal but valuable lesson. Never, ever take an audience for granted. Always do as much research as you can. A little bit of digging with a few simple questions could have created a completely different experience that morning. Remember, if you don't know, don't assume. Ask someone. I swore that I would do my utmost never to make the same mistake again. Over the years since, I've had a few wake-up calls, but thankfully I never have. [*Knock on wood*]

Find your Point A

There are many questions we can ask to ensure that we understand our audience. Let's focus on four of the most basic and most crucial.

- Who are they?
- What's going on with them?
- What's their level of knowledge?
- What's in it for them?

The answer to these questions forms your Point A. This point is the state of your audience *before* you begin presenting to them. It's their current state.

Who are they?

As you may have noticed in my previous story, I failed to answer this first basic question. I assumed that the storytelling and presentation skills audiences would essentially be the same. I was wrong. The second audience was larger, more personally ambitious, and far more experienced. As the APET team, they'd had plenty of professional development – everything from negotiation skills, in-depth psychometric profiling, resilience to wellness training. You name it. They knew what world-class development looked like and how it should be delivered.

When thinking about your audience, start by considering how many people will be attending and who they are. What are their demographics, psychographics, age, gender, seniority, experience, interests and commonalities? The more you understand them, the better your chance at connecting.

I often deliver essentially the same programme to vastly different audiences. Imagine the differences between an audience of sales managers from motor-vehicle dealerships and a group of creatives from an ad agency. Almost everything about them is different, from gender balance to educational background, political affiliations, ways of thinking, sense of humour and value systems. While the fundamental principles behind my content stay the same, the delivery of that content needs to flex and adapt to their different experiences and personalities.

What is going on with them?

Many of you will be delivering presentations that need to persuade. To do that effectively, you need to understand what's on your audience's minds. What problem is to be solved? Demonstrating that you recognise people's current concerns is a powerful place to begin to construct a persuasive message. What are they feeling at the start of the encounter, or what keeps them up at night? Are they uncertain and fearful and needing reassurance? Are they unmotivated and tired and need to be inspired? Are they feeling ignored and forgotten and need to be heard? What are their issues or concerns? What is their motivation?

When audiences hear you speak to their issues or concerns, empathise with them, be frustrated with them, hear their words articulated back to them, it builds trust and connection. Then, when you propose the solution or direction you wish to take them in, or the actions you want them to take, chances are your ability to persuade and motivate is improved. After all, why would I do anything you ask if I don't trust you or feel you understand me?

What's more, not all the issues or problems your audience faces may be obvious – even to them. There may be deeper, unspoken issues that people may be reluctant to admit. Tapping into these issues and providing solutions can be a powerful motivator for action.

What's their level of knowledge?

Knowing this ensures that your information is pitched at the correct level. Generally, audiences with a high level of expertise on your topic will be more open to you being granular with the detail. In fact, they may even expect it.

However, audiences with limited subject knowledge will quickly tune out if met with technical language, jargon and acronyms they don't understand. These audiences want simple, compelling ideas with plenty of stories they can relate to. As the previous story illustrates, another reason why my presentation went so poorly was that their level of knowledge around business storytelling was far more advanced than I had anticipated. The antithesis can be just as painful. Think how frustrating it is to listen to a presenter who speaks in complicated jargon or endless internal acronyms.

At times, the audience's level of knowledge may be quite varied. When that's the case, ensure you've identified the priority stakeholders or decision-makers in the room and seek a deeper understanding of their needs.

What is in it for them?

In other words, why should they listen to you? A good presenter should clearly articulate the value and benefit they bring to the audience. Consider how is your audience going to be different by the time they leave the room? What will they gain from the experience of your presentation?

Don't be afraid to ask your audience what they want from you.

A few years back, I coached a senior leader in operations within a major New Zealand corporate, who was asked to speak at a new conference specifically for women in operations. She'd received a brief from the conference organisers but felt it was off the mark in terms of value for her audience. So she called up six women she knew would be in the audience and asked what they most wanted to hear from her. Their responses gave her rich insight and a wonderful focus for her presentation. The post-conference feedback rated her talk as the highlight of the conference for many who attended. Why? Because she found a bridge between her experience and what was of interest to her audience. She started from a place of empathy and respect.

Presenting to executives

Executives and senior leaders can be a challenging crowd. Time is their most precious commodity, so don't waste it. Be succinct and get to the point. Furthermore, they're there to test your thinking so expect to be challenged and interrupted. In fact, a presentation to senior executives who pepper you with challenging questions is likely a good thing. It means they're engaged, interested and doing their job. Silence would be more of a worry.

Your first presentation to an executive team or board is one of the best opportunities to build your profile and reputation for competence. If ever there was a time for you to do your research and understand what your audience wants, then this is it.

Quick Tips: *Audience – Point A*

- Your audience is your priority. Disregard them at your peril.

- Find your Point A (the state of your audience before you begin presenting to them) with the following questions:

  1. Who are they? Demographics, psychographics, number of people, age, gender, experience level, interests, motivations, job position.

  2. What's going on with them? What are they worried about? What is their pain/pleasure? What's keeping them awake at night?

  3. What is their level of knowledge of your topic?

  4. What is in it for them? (Why should they listen to you? What value will they get from your presentation?)

Chapter Five

Your Objective – Point B

In the last chapter, we discussed Point A – where your audience is before your presentation begins. That is their current state. Your objective or Point B is where you want them to be by the end – their future state.

Put simply, the art of a great presentation is successfully moving your audience from their Point A to your Point B within the timeframe given. That's pretty much all there is to it. If you succeed in doing that (and if your Point B achieves the brief), you've delivered a successful presentation.

It's the outcome, not the process

The adage 'It's the journey that matters, not the destination' may be great philosophy for life, but presentations are all about the destination.

My second favourite question to ask a struggling presenter (after 'Who are you talking to?') is 'What is your objective?' Interestingly, they almost always respond with a description of what they will be talking about. Usually, it sounds a little like this: 'Hmmm...my objective...well first I want to talk about this thing, and then I'm gonna talk about this, and then this, and finally I'll cover off this.' The trouble is that this response focuses on what you're doing, not what you need your audience to do.

When they leave your presentation, your audience will be changed by their experience with you. Your objective defines what that change is. Are they adopting a new process? Understanding specific risks? Making an important decision? Having their minds changed? Whatever your message, be very clear on what success will look like for your audience.

Not having a clear objective is like trying to fly to a destination without the coordinates. Your presentation will have no direction, and you'll be off track and out of fuel in no time. Once we confirm our destination, we can ensure every piece of content is helping get our audience to that Point B. It's a wonderful way to help your content be relevant and targeted. Another way to think about it is to imagine your Points A and B as two foundations of a bridge that spans a great river. The goal of your presentation is to transport your audience to the other side.

As mentioned in the introduction, poor content drives poor delivery and ultimately keeps you in the shadows. Although it's usually your delivery skills, not content, that will get the blame. Too often, I see presenters communicating messages that are boring and irrelevant. Deep down, the presenter can feel this and that uncertainty fuels a hesitant and disconnected delivery. Starting your prep by defining your Point A and Point B will give you clarity and confidence. Even if you're called in to talk to a group with only ten minutes to prepare, quickly ask yourself, who are the people in the room and what do they really need from me? It will give you a reason to communicate.

Have a good reason why

If your presentation provides real value for your audience, then effectively communicating it becomes your duty. If there is no value, then perhaps you shouldn't be communicating at all. And that's completely fine. People default to a presentation before asking whether the message even needs to be delivered in that format. Perhaps you could achieve the same outcome with a quick conversation or a phone call? Take a moment to check whether a presentation is the best way to get the audience to your Point B? You may well be surprised at your answer. Perhaps it's not the best way. Terrific. The world now has one less pointless presentation. There are many methods of persuasion at your disposal. A presentation is not always the most effective.

Understanding Point B

There are three critical components to a great Point B – the Big Idea, the Outcome and the Obstacles.

The Big Idea

The Big Idea is the succinct articulation (think three sentences or less) of your core idea or insight. It should describe the current state or challenge, followed by the action or ask. Distilling your content into a single big idea can be challenging, but, in my experience, it is of great benefit to the coherence of your message.

Let's look at a well-crafted big idea across three different presentation scenarios.

Scenario 1: Third quarter financial update

Big Idea: Overall, our quarterly results are tracking as expected. However, a subtle but steady decrease in new accounts is signalling a softening market, so a re-think of our strategy will be necessary sooner than expected.

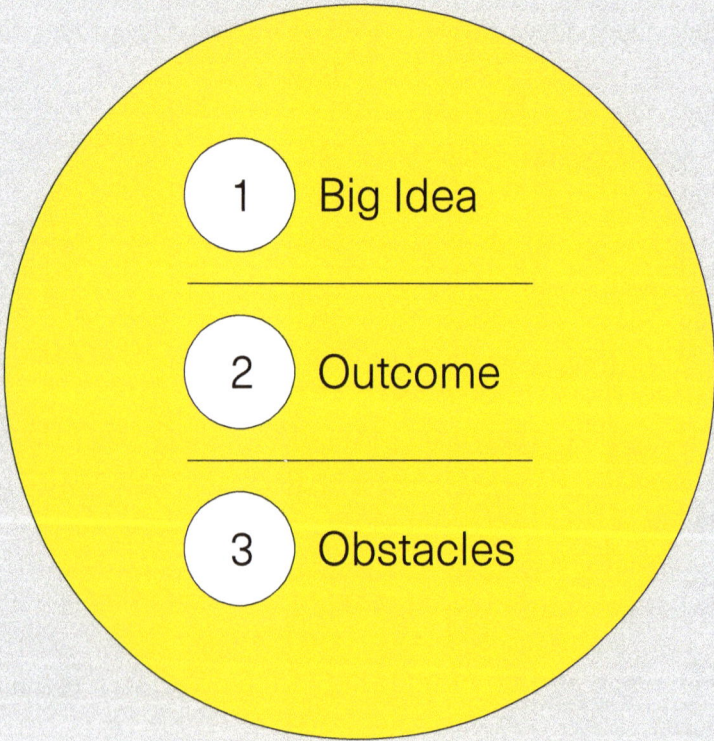

Figure 9: Your objective – Point B

Scenario 2: Power-plant turbine upgrade options

Big Idea: A failure in turbine three of our plant (which has now exceeded its operational lifespan) will be catastrophic to our customers and shareholders. Therefore, we must agree on one of the three upgrade options presented today.

Scenario 3: Marketing strategy rethink

Big Idea: Our marketing strategy is stuck in 2008. Seventy-eight per cent of our marketing budget is spent on print and radio, while sixty-two per cent of new leads come from our digital channels. What's more, the acquisition cost of those leads is half that of our traditional channels. To stay relevant and reach our customers, we need to engage a specialist digital agency to help to re-think our whole marketing strategy.

The Outcome

The second component of your Point B is The Outcome which I define as what you want your audience to think, feel, and do. Be specific and realistic with your answer to the following three questions.

By the end of the presentation...

What do you want your audience to *think*?

What do you want them to *feel*?

What do you want them to *do*?

Check to ensure the outcome you've decided upon is achievable within the available time. Here are examples building on the three scenarios above.

Scenario 1: Third quarter financial update

Think: The emerging trend is credible, and it is prudent to anticipate a softening market and be proactive in our strategic response to a potential downturn.

Feel: Concerned and motivated to act.

Do: Agree to bring the strategic review forward to next month – six months earlier than anticipated.

Scenario 2: Power-plant turbine upgrade options

Think: Understand the time for action is now, and doing nothing is no longer an option.

Feel: A sense of urgency to act and confidence in the robustness of the analysis underpinning each option.

Do: Approve the move forward on one of the three options presented.

Scenario 3: Marketing strategy rethink

Think: Recognise the world has moved on and that the current marketing spend is based on flawed logic and weighted toward the wrong channels.

Feel: Be confident and secure that a new digital focus will yield better sales with more efficiency and without cannibalising too many leads from traditional channels.

Do: Agree to engage an agency and re-allocate fifty per cent of the three-month marketing spend away from print and radio into the proposed three-month digital focus trial.

The Obstacles

The final part of setting a clear objective is identifying why your audience might not want to go to your Point B. Anticipating the obstacles from your audience will significantly increase your chances of successful outcomes. The more you understand these, the better chance you have of navigating around them.

Generally, your obstacles are:

- Rational – costs involved, limited resources, competing priorities

- Emotional – misconceptions, biases, moral codes, misinformation

- Situational – fatigued audiences, noisy or distracting environments

- Personal – your reputation, integrity, likeability.

Here are some example obstacles for the three scenarios above.

Scenario 1: Third quarter financial update

- Conflicting data from another part of the organisation that suggests a market improvement
- Lack of trust in your expertise because you're young, new in the organisation and lack credibility
- 'Old dog' egos who say they've seen this all before and there's nothing to worry about.

Scenario 2: Power-plant turbine upgrade options

- Lack of cashflow for capital maintenance
- Conflicting or competing capital expenditure priorities

- Lack of trust in the robustness of your analysis due to a reputation for a lack of attention to detail.

Scenario 3: Marketing strategy rethink

- Limited knowledge and trust around the efficacy of digital channels

- Entrenched opinions

- A distracted and sabotaging GM who sees your advocacy and ideas as a direct threat to their job security.

Once you've explored and identified your big idea, your outcome and your obstacles, you have your Point B: What you want your audience to think, feel or do about your big idea, and how to navigate around any obstacles on the way.

Keep perspective

You won't always achieve your desired outcome no matter how brilliant you are or how terrific your presentation is. That's ok. Every presenter will occasionally fail to make their case or get buy-in from their audience. Maybe somebody else's idea is a better way forward for the organisation, or perhaps the budget just isn't there for your new idea. Just because you don't achieve your objective does not mean your presentation is unsuccessful.

The larger point at play is the value derived from the powerful contesting of ideas. Remember, it's the creation, communication and successful execution of great ideas that drive organisations forward and change the world. Advocating to the best of your ability increases the chances of ideas being picked up and acted upon.

Quick Tips: *Objective – Point B*

- Develop your Objective or Point B. This is where you want your audience to be by the end of your presentation. It has three components: Big Idea, Outcome and Obstacles.

- Craft your Big Idea – a succinct articulation (think three sentences or less) of your core idea or insight. It should describe the current state or challenge, followed by the action or ask.

- Clarify your Outcome – Know what do you want your audience to think, feel and do by the end of the presentation. Be specific. Make sure it's realistic and achievable.

- Identify your Obstacles. How might your audience resist moving to Point B. These obstacles could be rational, emotional, situational or personal.

- Remember, a great presentation will navigate your obstacles and successfully transport your audience from their Point A (current state) to your Point B (future state).

Chapter Six

The Structure

Well organised content will take your audience from Point A to Point B, so the next step is creating a solid structure that supports your content. Earlier, I likened Point A and Point B to the foundations of a bridge, so now think of your presentation structure as the great span of steel girders that support the journey across.

Business and organisational presentations usually fall under two broad types – Informative or Persuasive.

Informative presentations include updates, reports, training, progress reports and the like, while persuasive types involve pitches, sales, persuading, motivating and inspiring. This chapter will cover different structural options – some appropriate for informative and some for persuasive presentations. But before we delve into them, let's talk about the power of the three-part pattern.

The three-part pattern

Audiences love information that follows predictable and recognisable patterns. These help us draw links between ideas and build a sense of narrative. The three-part pattern structure is simple and powerful, and when you start looking, it's everywhere. From Aristotle's three-acts (beginning, middle and end) to religious iconography and even fairy tales (think the Three Little Pigs or Goldilocks and the Three

Bears), the three-part pattern has helped humans process information and story for thousands of years.

This should be the first structural pattern to master for every good presenter, and it will be a great default option for most of your presentations. As Toyota is to motor vehicles, the three-part pattern is to presentation structure – practical, reliable and good to learn with.

Let's look at a few examples:

Three-part pattern examples

Topical: Point 1, Point 2, Point 3

Type: Informative/Persuasive

Good for: Almost anything. A simple, versatile structure.
               A great default option.

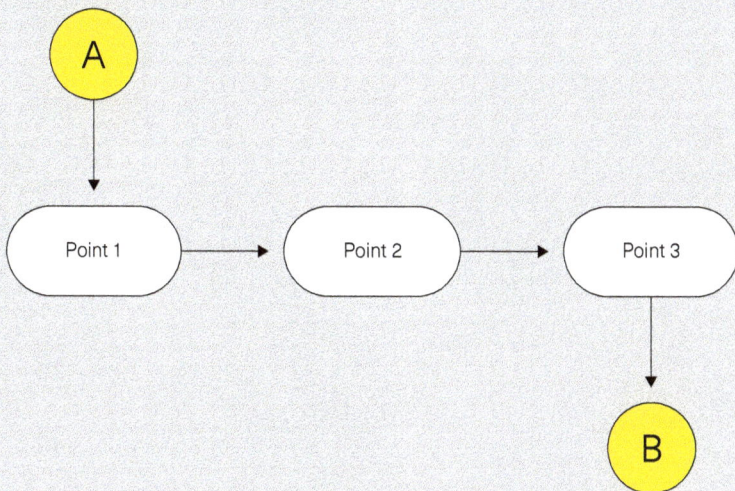

Figure 10: Three-part pattern

Information: What? So what? Now what?

Type: Informative

Good for: Sharing information, general updating.

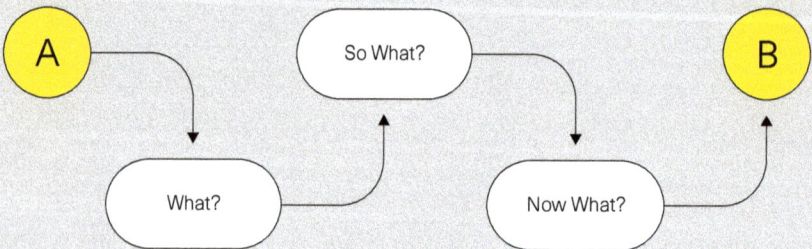

Figure 11: Information: What? So what? Now what?

Why: Why? How? What?

Type: Informative/Persuasive

Good for: Explaining a new process, outlining a shift in direction.

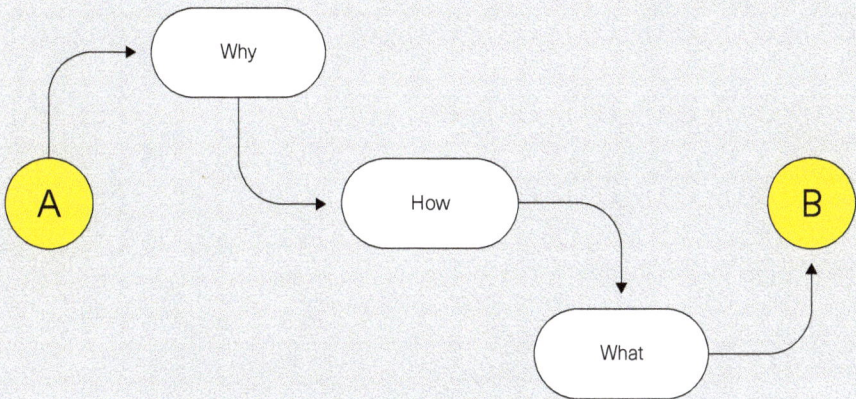

Figure 12: Why: Why? How? What?

Historical: Past, Present, Future

Type: Informative

Good for: Financial or KPI updates, historical context.

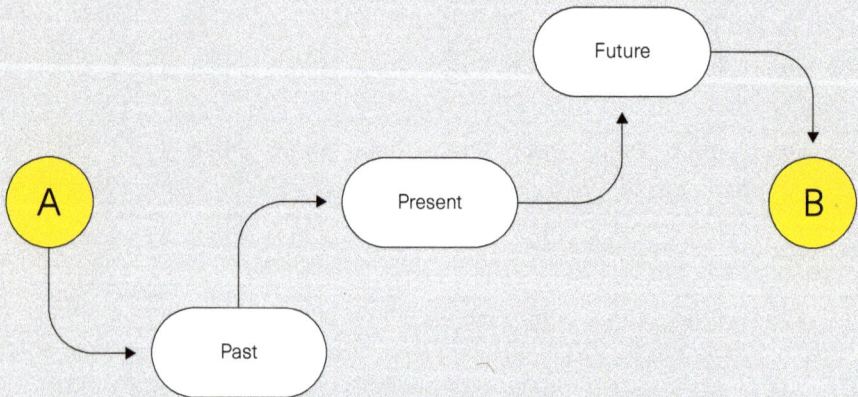

Figure 13: Historical: Past, Present, Future

Instruct: First, you do this, then do this, then this.

Type: Informative

Good for: Building capability, instructing,
             sequential process training.

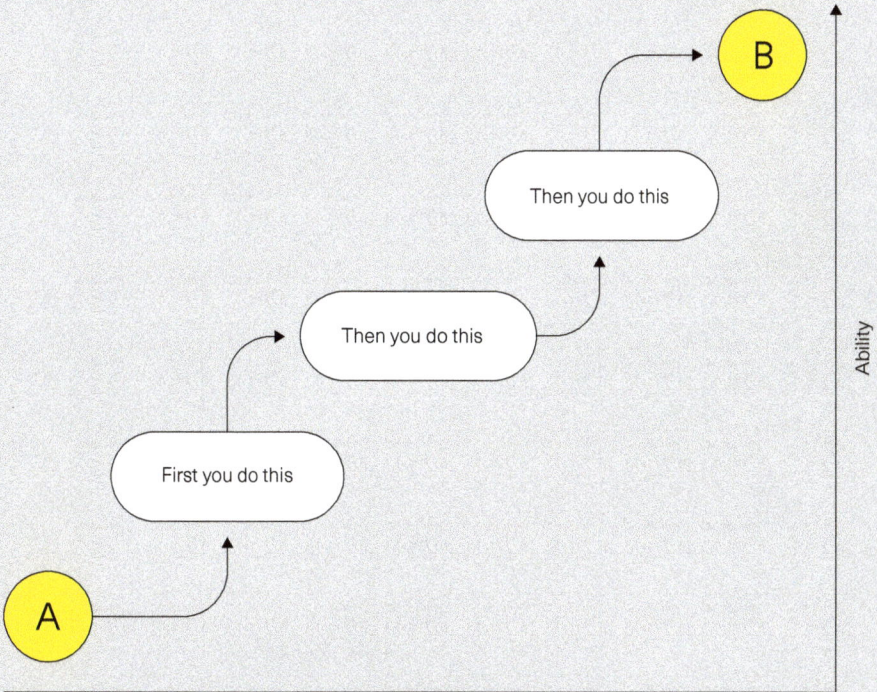

Figure 14: Instruct: First, you do this, then do this, then this

Problem: Problem, Solution(s), Recommendation

Type: Persuasive

Good for: Presenting business cases, proposals.

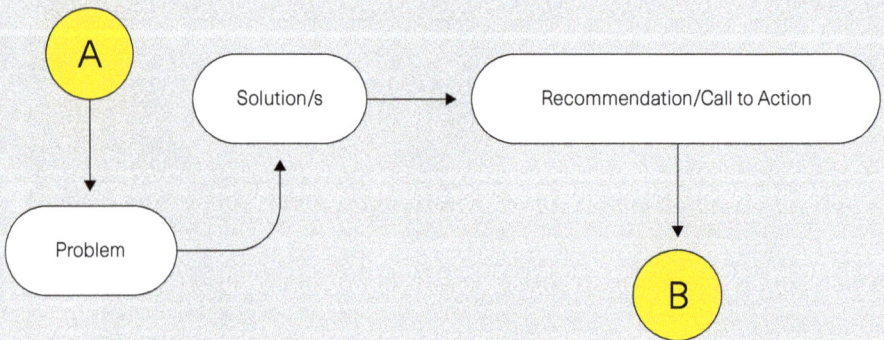

Figure 15: Problem: Problem, Solution(s), Recommendation

Other useful structures:

Numerical (the listicle):

Type: Informative

Good for: External presentations to large, general audiences.

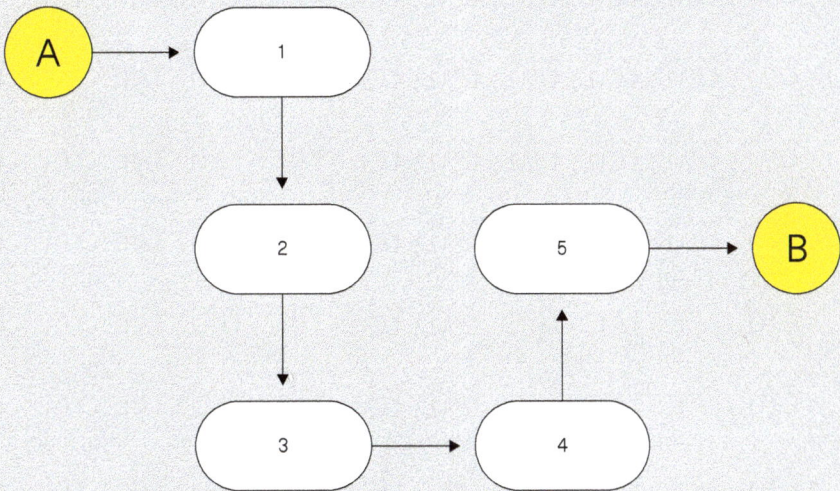

Figure 16: Numerical (the listicle)

Why change: How things were... Complication... Adaptation (new current state)... Future state

Type: Persuasive

Good for: Unveiling a new strategy or explaining the why behind change.

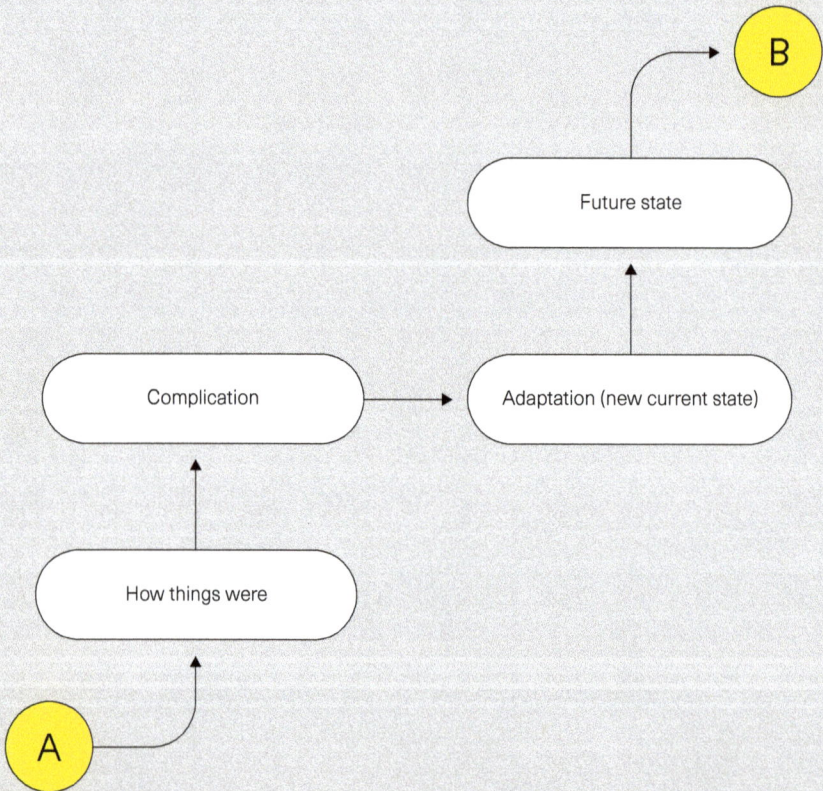

Figure 17: Why change

Pitch

Good for: Pitching, capital raising

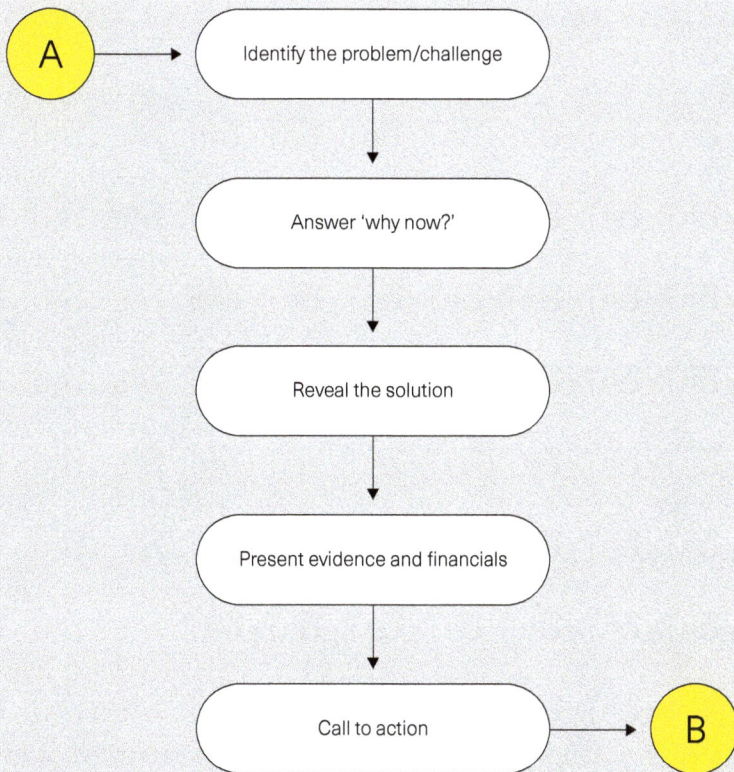

Figure 18: Pitch

The following are some sample structures for the three presentation scenarios explored in the previous chapter.

Scenario 1: Third quarter financial update

Big Idea: Overall, our quarterly results are tracking as expected. However, a subtle but steady decrease in new accounts is signalling a softening market, so a re-think of our strategy will be necessary sooner than expected.

Potential Structure: Topical

Point 1: Re-cap on Quarter 3 performance

Point 2: Analysis of emerging trends

Point 3: Recommendations and discussion

Scenario 2: Power-plant turbine upgrade options

Big Idea: A failure in turbine three of our plant (which has now exceeded its operational lifespan) will be catastrophic to our customers and shareholders. Therefore it's critical that we agree on one of the three upgrade options presented today.

Potential Structure: Problem/Solution

Problem: Overview of Turbine 3 challenge

Solution/s: Three different maintenance options – risks vs. rewards

Recommendation: Recommended option + discussion.

Scenario 3: Marketing Strategy rethink

Big Idea: Our marketing strategy is stuck in 2008. Seventy-eight per cent of our marketing budget is spent on print and radio, but sixty-two per cent of new leads come from our digital channels.

What's more, the acquisition cost of those leads is half that of our traditional channels. To stay relevant and reach our customers, we need to engage a specialist digital agency to help to re-think our whole marketing strategy.

Potential Structure: Why change

How things were: How marketing used to work for us

Complication: Why it now doesn't. The disruption and opportunity of digital

Adaptation: What we now need to change to harness this opportunity

Future State: What success will look like and how we'll measure.

Quick Tips: *Structure*

- Your structure will bridge the gap between Point A and Point B and support your content.

- A recognisable pattern in your structure will support your narrative and help your audience comprehend and engage with your message.

- Consider your structure based on whether your presentation is more informative or persuasive.

- The three-part-pattern should be your default presentation structure – think three key points.

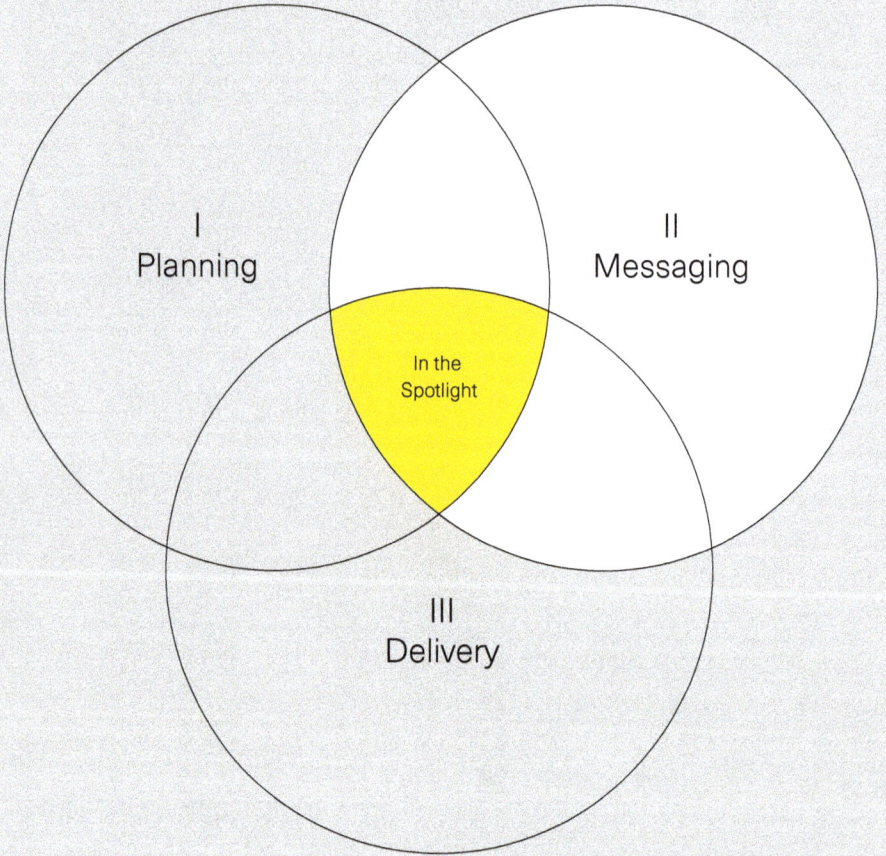

Section II
Messaging

Chapter Seven

The Open and Close

The Opening is Everything

Many years ago at drama school, I heard a quote attributed to the great Shakespearean actor, Sir Lawrence Olivier, highlighting the importance of stepping on stage with intention: 'If you don't grab your audience in the first thirty seconds, you'll never have them!'

But all is not lost if you don't manage to grip your audience with Shakespearean intensity immediately, although undoubtedly, the first three minutes of any presentation are the most important. That is when your audience will form many of their assumptions about you and your message.

Much needs to happen in those moments. An audience needs to see relevance and value in what you're going to say, they need to be introduced to who you are and your credibility, and they need to know why they are listening to you and where you will be taking them. I love to see a presenter effortlessly start their presentation and make me feel like they've truly got this and that I'm in safe hands. So, start as you mean to go on.

Your opening should achieve four crucial tasks:

- Create impact
- Introduce you and establish your credibility
- Communicate the purpose of the presentation
- Lay out a road map as to where you will be taking your audience

Task One: Create impact

Your goal at the start is to hook your audience with something that motivates them to listen to you. You may choose to introduce yourself first (task two) if that feels more appropriate.

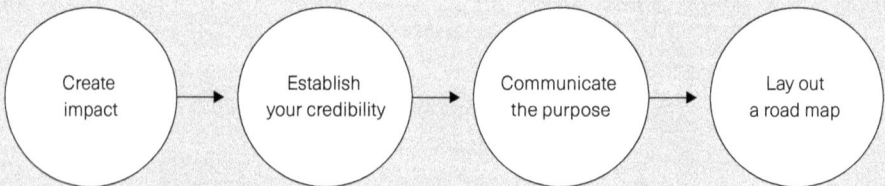

Figure 19: The Open

Here are some techniques to open with impact and make those three minutes count. Remember, keep it relevant to your topic and watch out for being gimmicky or cheesy. The opening needs to feel effortless and natural to an audience, rather than obvious or 'presentery.'

A relevant story

In her amazing TED talk, *The Power Of Vulnerability*, Brené Brown begins with a story about an event planner refusing to call her a researcher because it sounded boring.[1] Instead, the planner wanted to describe her as a storyteller. Brown, an academic qualitative researcher, recoiled from this airy-fairy label and drew deep on her courage to compromise on 'researcher-storyteller.'

Brown allows us to see the vulnerability she felt at having her identity and credentials under fire, but at the same time ensures we know what her formal credentials are. In less than a minute, she establishes her expertise, authority and empathy using warm, self-deprecating humour that charms us into paying attention. It's an excellent example of opening with a story.

Avoid saying things like: 'Let me start with a story...'. That will likely get you eye rolls. A good rule of thumb is, when telling a story, don't mention it's a story. Look at the storytelling section in Chapter Nine for tips on crafting a good story.

A question

Questions can be terrific at grabbing your audience's attention. 'Can I see a show of hands? How many people believe the presentations they gave earlier in their career could have been a lot better with some decent training?' The objective here is to promote interaction. A question gets the audience thinking rather than judging you. A word of caution, though, don't start with a question if you're unsure how your audience will respond.

A compelling fact or statistic

'Over the past twelve quarters, we've seen an average increase in sales of one to two per cent. Since executing our new sales strategy, this last quarter has seen sales increase by twenty-eight per cent. That's a remarkable result.'

When used well, a compelling fact or statistic, whether celebratory or shocking, can be a great emotional hook.

A quote

Jerry Seinfeld put it nicely: 'According to most studies, people's number one fear is public speaking. Number two is death. Death is number two! Does that sound right? This means to the average person, if you go to a funeral, you're better off in the casket than doing the eulogy.' Be sure to use quotes that you and your audience can genuinely relate to – rather than ones that just make you look smart.

A puzzle

Psychologist Adam Grant advocates intellectual puzzles to get your audience focused on your ideas rather than on you. 'Why is it that something as natural and easy as speaking becomes so difficult as soon as we stand up in front of an audience?[2]

Define the problem or dilemma

'Team, we have a problem....'

Mining your obstacles

I love this technique. If you're struggling to think of a compelling opening, go back to your notes from Step Three and identify the biggest obstacle you face in moving your audience to your Point B.

Now, see if you can focus on immediately destroying or debunking that obstacle with a powerful opening statement.

Task Two: Introduce yourself and establish your credibility

If it makes you more comfortable, introducing yourself first, before creating impact, is completely fine. It's your choice – just remember that it's the predictable choice – and you don't always want to be predictable.

If your audience already knows you and sees you as credible, then skip this step.

In a business environment, the easiest way to phrase your introduction is: 'For those of you who don't know me, my name is _____.' - then add here a few sentences on why you're qualified to speak on the topic.

Know your Pepeha

If your work is based in New Zealand, particularly with Iwi or in the public sector, you should know how to speak your Pepeha. It is a way of introducing yourself in Te Reo Māori that tells the story of the people and places you are connected to. It's more and more common to see presenters begin with their Pepeha. If you don't already know yours, you can visit pepeha.nz for a guide to creating it. Be sure to check with the host in regards to tikanga (correct protocol) and what else may be required from you.

Task Three: Purpose statement

Your purpose statement is one or two sentences that you should state after your impact opening and introduction. It should define what you are talking about and how it will help them. If relevant, it should also include the 'ask' – which is what you're asking your audience to do, consider or approve. However, if your ask (or topic) is highly contentious, you may want to save it till the end after you've made your case.

The simplest form of this statement is:

'The purpose of my presentation today is to...'

Other forms could be:

'What I'm here to talk about today is....'

'I'm here today to....'

'By the end of this presentation, my goal is....'

'My purpose for being here today is....'

'If there's one thing I want you to take away from this presentation, it's this....'

Sometimes your purpose statement may include the Big Idea part of the outcome (think, feel, do) you've set for yourself in your Point B – and that's completely fine. At other times, say in sales encounters, you may wish to keep the desired outcome private as you could risk seeming assumptive or manipulative.

For example, if I was giving an initial presentation to a prospective client on why they should use The Pickering Group's programmes, my outcome (do) could be: *'To get this prospect to commit to a pilot of a two-day training course.'*

But my purpose statement should align with their needs and how I can help them: *'The purpose of this presentation is to introduce you to The Pickering Group's suite of development programmes and share with you how we can support your people to be more impactful, engaging presenters.'*

Task Four: Your roadmap

Before you move into the main body of the presentation, it's important to give the audience a roadmap of where they'll be heading. Starting your presentation with the general outline of what to expect before proceeding into more detail will greatly help audience comprehension. Outline the key points by telling them what you're going to tell them. If necessary, also include here:

- A time signature – how long the presentation will take. Very important.

- When they can ask questions

- Any handouts available

- Break times.

Putting it all together

Let's look at a quick example. Say you're a Learning & Development manager looking to convince your leadership team to implement a presentation skills development programme for the sales team. The opening, including all four tasks, could sound like this:

Good morning team.

The recent productivity survey of our sales team has produced some worrying statistics. Seventy-five per cent of them feel ill-equipped and lack confidence when presenting to large audiences, and more than fifty per cent feel we've lost deals purely due to poor presentation skills. What's more, we know many of the team will be expected to present and represent the company at industry events over the next twelve months.

[Introduce yourself and your position here]

The purpose of my presentation today is to walk you through the benefits and costs of adding a solid presentation skills programme to our regular L&D offering and to seek approval to run an initial pilot programme.

I'm going to cover three key points:

1. *Why presentation skills are now our primary learning priority.*

2. *The available development programmes, cost analysis and my recommendation.*

3. *Pilot programme details and proposed time frame for roll-out.*

The presentation will be about fifteen minutes, but because we're pushed for time, I'd ask you to save questions until the end. I have also prepared detailed handouts, which I'll provide to you before you leave.

There you have it: a simple opening detailing where you're heading and deliverable in less than a minute. Remember, don't memorise it like a script. Keep it conversational.

The close wraps it up

Just like your opening, your close should achieve four tasks.

Summary: Summarise your main points

Conclusion/Call to action: State your conclusion – if you can frame it as a call to action, even better. Make sure this statement aligns with your purpose statement.

Q&A: If necessary, your Q&A session should come next. I don't recommend that you end with Q&A unless you're doing an executive summary. We'll cover Q&As in more detail in Chapter Eleven.

Impact (optional): Thank them and leave them with something impactful. Link your close to your opening. You may wish to memorise your final few sentences to ensure you end dynamically and professionally. You could try something like: 'That's all the time we have for questions. Let me leave you with this...'

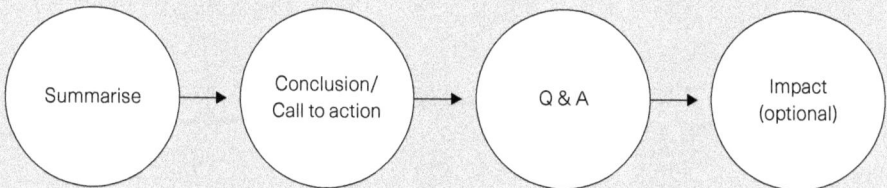

Summarise → Conclusion/ Call to action → Q & A → Impact (optional)

Figure 20: The Close

In summary, I've covered three main points today:

- The key benefits to the company of introducing this programme
- Offerings and costs
- Proposed time frame for the pilot rollout.

I trust I've effectively highlighted the many ongoing benefits a solid presentation development offering can bring to our sales team and, if approved today, how we will roll out an initial pilot offering.

We have ten minutes for questions, if there are any? Fire away...

[Q&A]

I want to leave you with a final thought: Of the seventy-five per cent of our sales team who struggle when presenting to large audiences, every single one felt that with proper training they could significantly exceed their sales targets each quarter. They are hungry to do better for our company; all they need now is your support. Thank you very much for your time.

Quick Tips: *The Open and Close*

- Creating your opening and close at this point will help make your core content more efficient to assemble and relevant for your audience.

- The first three minutes of your presentation are the most important. Make them count.

- Your opening should achieve four crucial tasks:

  - Create impact

  - Introduce you and establish your credibility

  - Communicate the purpose of the presentation and the ask (if relevant)

  - Lay out a road map of where you will be taking your audience. Include an outline of your main points and a time signature.

- Your close should:

  - Summarise your main points

  - Have a clear conclusion and call to action (if needed)

  - Leave time for a Q&A (if you're not allowing for questions throughout).

Chapter Eight

Your Core Content

The Heart of the Matter

It's time to create and assemble your core content. The role of content is to transport your audience from their Point A to your Point B. Core Content is everything you will say – the words you will speak, the argument you make, the evidence you show, and the case studies you share. It is the stories you tell, the ideas you espouse, the proposals you propose, and the demonstrations you give. Because you've already decided on your overarching structure and created your opening and close, creating and assembling your content should be relatively straightforward. Keep it simple and avoid unnecessary jargon.

Beware the curse of knowledge – when you're very knowledgeable about a topic, it can be more challenging to communicate simply because the context is obvious to you. Remember, your audience is likely hearing this information for the first time.

For your content to be compelling, it needs to resonate with and be relevant to your audience. That's why it's crucial to constantly ask yourself: 'Will this piece of content help transport my audience to my Point B? Is it relevant and interesting to them?' If the answer is no, then it shouldn't be in your presentation.

The pillars of persuasion

More than two thousand years ago, the Greek philosopher Aristotle and his fellow polymaths had already figured out what people needed to be persuasive when speaking. His theory still forms the basis of many books you'll read on persuasive communication or public speaking. The theory is commonly called The Three Pillars of Persuasion, and these pillars are ethos, pathos and logos. Aristotle said we must have elements of all three to be persuasive in our arguments (and our presentations).

Ethos: This is your credibility or character. Does your audience respect you and trust you? Do they believe you're an expert? This is often established before you even enter the room or through your introduction. Ethos is reinforced throughout your presentation when your audience experiences you delivering well and inspiring confidence.

Pathos: This is the heart; it's your emotional connection with your audience. Are you appealing to the emotions of your audience?

Logos: And finally, your head, or the logical argument. Does your presentation make sense? Is it based on facts and evidence?

From Aristotle's model, we can divide core content into two broad categories: Rational and Emotive.

Rational content

This is your use of logical reasoning, expertise and data to inform or persuade others. Whatever your level, this is a critical skill to master. Organisations need to make their decisions on the best evidence they can muster. Consider the following. Is your content well-structured and easy to follow? Do you understand, and can you explain, the financial implications of your proposal or project? Can you simplify

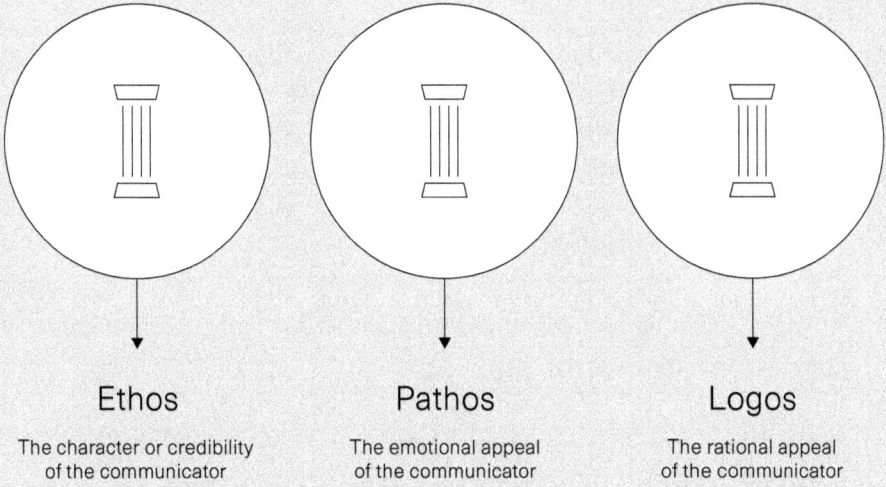

Ethos

The character or credibility
of the communicator

Pathos

The emotional appeal
of the communicator

Logos

The rational appeal
of the communicator

Figure 21: Aristotle's pillars of persuasion

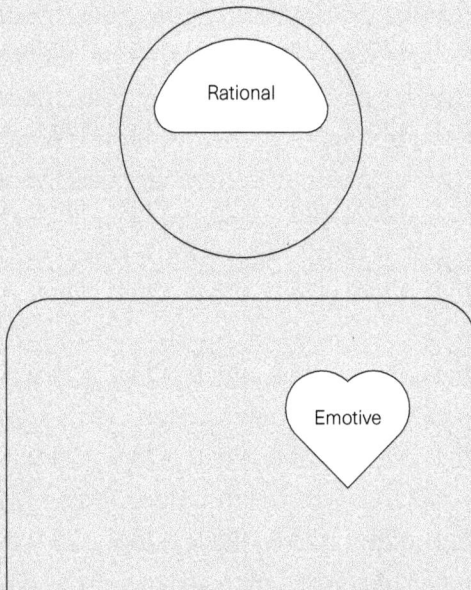

Rational

Emotive

Figure 22: The two types of content

and communicate relevant and valuable insight from disparate and complex datasets?

Your rational content will include facts, figures, costs, proof, timings, numbers, calculations, evidence, case studies, research, results, forecasts, predictions and analyses.

Framing and anchoring

These are simple psychology-based tools that can make rational content even more persuasive.

Framing: Research from cognitive psychologists Daniel Kahneman and Amos Tversky shows we can influence people toward more risk-seeking or risk-averse behaviours by setting the context for particular ideas or proposals. When an option is framed as a gain we become *risk-averse*, and when framed as a loss, we may become *risk-seeking*.[1]

Say you are making an argument for entering a new market. To frame it as a gain (and make the audience more risk-averse), you could say, 'We should enter this market because we can grow eleven per cent in market share.' Framed as a loss (making the audience more risk-seeking), you might say, 'By not entering into this market, we are missing out on the opportunity to grow eleven per cent in market share.' The shift is subtle, but Kahneman and Tversky's research shows this will make your statement more persuasive. Facts, figures, and analyses matter, of course, but so does how you frame the content for your audience.

Anchoring: This is based on research showing that when an initial estimate is on the table (whether budget, cost, or growth), people will anchor to that initial estimate and only adjust incrementally off that starting value.[2] It describes our tendency to rely heavily on the first piece of information offered. For example, say you're pitching a business case for a substantial increase in your IT budget. Taking a low anchor position, you could open your case with 'Our last year's IT budget was $1.5 million.' Or, taking a high anchor position, you could start with 'Our top competitor's average IT budget is around $2.3 million.' The high anchor will likely help you win a bigger increase.

Emotive content

Emotive content is everything that has emotional resonance with people. Stories are your most powerful tool of persuasion. Every effective communicator you know is likely a good storyteller, yet many presenters are still uncomfortable using stories to convince and persuade. Their presentations are heavy on facts and figures, and light on anything that triggers any emotional response.

Stories are simply the best mechanism to create pathos. You can also use analogy, metaphor and other figures of speech to help generate an emotional connection and explain ideas or concepts.

So, what exactly is a story?

Legendary screenwriting teacher Robert McKee defines it well, saying, 'A story expresses how and why life changes.'[3] Therefore, a good *business* story expresses how and why *a business* changes.

Stories work for three main reasons:

- They are memorable
- They create meaning
- They drive action.

As historian Yuval Noah Harari notes, our unique ability to construct and believe in fiction is the single biggest characteristic that underpins the collective dominance of humankind.[4] Stephen King calls it telepathy: the power of a story to take an image from an author's head and effortlessly place it in the heads of others.[5] Storytelling is a powerful tool. A successful presentation contains a balance of rational and emotive content, and the best emotive tool you have is to tell a story.

How to find your spotlight stories

You don't have to be Stephen King. In fact it's best if you're not, because your stories should be business-appropriate, not terrifying. Focus on small stories or anecdotes that help emphasise a business point. I call these Spotlight Stories because they're short, highly illuminating and a key characteristic of being 'in the spotlight.' They usually come from your practical experience: authentic snapshots of innovation, leadership, principles, customer service, vision, resilience, success, failure, courage, curiosity – you name it. And they've got an unexpected twist and a relevant point to make.

Five essentials of a spotlight story

1. **Setting:** When and where the story took place. This helps the audience to picture the scenario and ties it into reality. Just as 'Once upon a time' sets up a mythical distant past, 'Last week in Wellington...' establishes a concrete setting.

2. **Characters:** Every story needs characters who act. These will be the real people of your experience and what they did and said that created the story. It's this interaction between people that will give your stories a good sense of drama.

3. **Consequence:** One thing leads to another. We create meaning with stories by showing how events link to each other, such as 'the goat ate it, then because of that...' This creates a sense of flow and narrative – like the plot of a novel or film.

4. **The Twist:** Every good story contains an element of surprise. A story without one is anticlimactic and feels pointless, so

the end of your story needs some kind of reveal that justifies telling the tale.

5. **Relevance:** The story must support your message in some way. If it isn't relevant to your presentation, doesn't elucidate or emphasise any business point, then there's no reason to include it.

The right tale for the right ears

Ask yourself these four questions:

What point does this story make or reinforce?

Is it compelling?

Is it relevant?

At what point should I tell it for the best impact?

Different audiences will have different tolerance to stories. While stories can illustrate a complicated concept to fresh ears, an audience already familiar with that concept may find it patronising or pointless. But as we saw with Brené Brown, a story can also illustrate you, or create a sense of urgency or celebration. The key is to make sure your story is appropriate for your audience.

An example

In what has become the most-watched TED talk of all time, *'Why Schools Kill Creativity,'* the late Sir Ken Robinson tells the story of Gillian, a little girl who couldn't sit still at school. Her teachers were frustrated, and she was sent to a specialist for assessment.

After speaking with Gillian, the specialist asked her mother to leave the room with him. As they went, he switched on the radio. As soon as she was alone, the little girl started moving to the music. The

 Setting

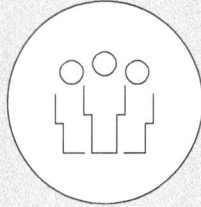 Characters

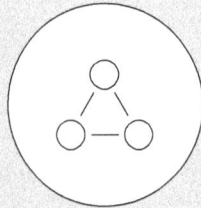 Consequence

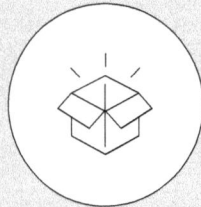 Twist

 Relevance

Figure 23: Five essentials of a spotlight story

specialist said, 'Mrs Lynne, Gillian's not sick – she's a dancer.' Her mother sensibly sent her to dance school, and Gillian became a successful dancer, then a choreographer for Andrew Lloyd-Webber.

A less fortunate child might have been medicated, punished, or written off as a lost cause, but Gillian's natural abilities (liabilities in a traditional classroom) made her rich, famous and fulfilled. Robinson uses many stories throughout his talk but leaves his most powerful story until near the end. It has the five essentials of a Spotlight Story - and its placement, relevance and authenticity, reinforces his big idea far more effectively than any PowerPoint full of facts and figures.[6]

Other types of emotive content

Analogy and metaphor

Figures of speech help you tap into an emotional connection and explain ideas or concepts. Perhaps you noticed that I used the metaphor of a bridge spanning a river to illustrate the importance of Point A and Point B.

If you were giving a speech on gang violence in your city, you could start by plainly stating, 'We have a problem in our city with gang violence.' A more emotive option could be to use a metaphor: 'Gang violence is a cancer, killing our city. We must eradicate it...'. A tad dramatic, but you get the idea.

Familiar phrases like 'stay in your bubble,' 'big bang,' 'cold feet,' or 'fish out of water' are all metaphors. Analogies are particularly useful when explaining something complex to audiences with limited subject knowledge. It is saying something is like something else to explain a point. For example, I could turn my 'bridge over a river' metaphor into an analogy by saying, 'Imagine your Point A and Point B as the foundations of a bridge that transports your audience from one side to another. If either foundation is weak or missing, your audience could tip into the swirling current and be washed away.'

Demonstrations and props

Physical demonstrations and props can work brilliantly to make a point. Say, for example, you are a computer manufacturer, and you want to convince the CIO of a large engineering firm to invest in your new super-robust tablet. You could show screeds of scientific test data to back up your claim, or you could stand on a chair and drop the tablet to the ground. Imagine their delight when you proceed to show that it still works perfectly. Just be sure to test your demonstration well in your practise.

Some will be aware of the infamous glass-testing demonstration with the live-stream launch of Tesla's cyber-truck. A heavy ball-bearing swung against the glass, supposedly to demonstrate the toughness and strength. However, the glass shattered – not once but twice! Tesla later claimed the demonstration had worked perfectly in their practise. However, the truck windows were slightly ajar during the live launch, causing unanticipated flex and the ultimate shattering.

Emotive visual aids

Well-chosen and good quality images are terrific for enabling an emotional connection with your audience. The introduction of warning pictures on cigarette packets is a perfect example. Health authorities know that showing a picture of a diseased lung is far more effective than just stating in writing that smoking causes lung cancer. We'll cover this in-depth in Chapter Ten.

The reveal

The precise moment when something new – a powerful idea, an amazing new product, a revolutionary service – is revealed to an audience is a powerful emotional trigger. Steve Jobs was a master of the reveal, as is Elon Musk – despite the cyber-truck fail. Creating anticipation then delighting or surprising is worthy of exploration.

Humour

When used appropriately, humour can be wonderful and engaging. However, you don't need to try to be funny to deliver a terrific presentation. If humour sits naturally with you, then, by all means, use it. If, however, your humour seems inauthentic, inappropriate or contrived, it can fall flat or even offend. There's nothing worse than crickets where there's supposed to be hysterics. So remember, your audience may not have the same sense of humour as you – chances are you're not the next Wanda Sykes – so use with caution and test before you try.

Slogans and quotes

From Obama's 'Yes we can!' to Ardern's 'They are us', slogans are powerful devices when they truly resonate with an audience.

Filtering and refining

Once you've generated your content, undertake a process of filtering and refining. Less is more. Be ruthless. Remove any idea that does not propel your audience to your Point B. At this stage (not before), it's important to remember the golden rule of assembling information for presentations: As little as possible, as much as necessary. Filter to the essence.

And remember, a great presentation must have the appropriate balance of both rational and emotive content types.

Managing attention spans

Our brains need a break

On average, the human brain will pay attention for only ten minutes before concentration falls away dramatically – even when the presenter is connected, and the topic is relevant. We can effectively combat this with state changes.

Take a look at the graph below. You'll notice that it takes around three minutes before you have the full attention of the audience. That's why beginning your presentation with a real attention grabber is so effective.

State changes

A state change is when you introduce a shift in your presentation to create interest and maintain the attention of your audience. Let's say your presentation is fifty minutes. Chunking it into ten-minute sections and allowing for a state change before or after each section will significantly increase your audience's ability to remain focused on your message. Effective state changes can be as simple as telling a relevant story or anecdote, interacting in groups to discuss a topic, changing speakers, having a break, showing a video or handing around a prop or sample.

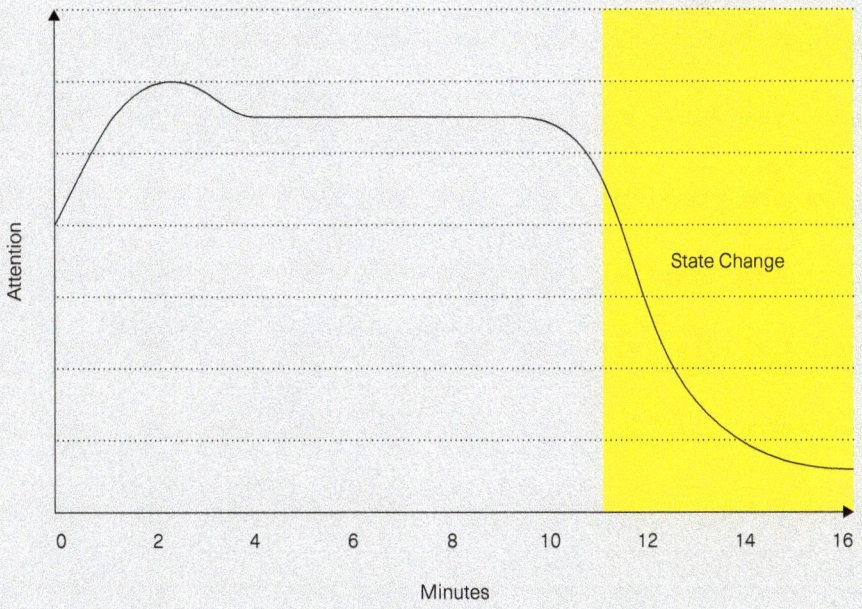

Figure 24: Attention spans and state changes

Quick Tips: *Core Content*

- The role of your core content is to transport your audience from Point A to Point B.

- Your core content should consist of two main types, rational and emotive.

- Rational is your logical reasoning, your evidence and your argument, e.g. facts, figures, costs, timing, proof, evidence, examples.

- Emotive content should not be neglected. Include (where appropriate) stories, anecdotes, analogies, metaphor, demonstrations and props.

- Remember, stories are your most powerful tool of persuasion. Include them.

- As a rule of thumb: For audiences with high subject knowledge, use more rational content. Audiences with limited subject knowledge need more emotive content.

Chapter Nine

Visual Aids

'People who know what they're talking about don't need PowerPoint.
– Steve Jobs

Death by PowerPoint

Yale University professor Edward R. Tufte put it best when he used a drug analogy to critique the prevalence of slideware (PowerPoint and Keynote) in business and education.

'Imagine a widely used and expensive prescription drug that promised to make us beautiful but didn't. Instead, the drug had frequent, serious side effects. It induced stupidity, turned everyone into bores, wasted time, and degraded the quality and credibility of communication. These side effects would rightly lead to a worldwide product recall.'[1]

Millions of PowerPoint presentations are made across the globe every day. But rather than aiding presentations, PowerPoint has become a substitute, offering a crutch to the presenter and often confusion and boredom to their audience. One of the biggest hindrances to impactful presentations is the way most people use visual aid software.

The same problems consistently arise whether on PowerPoint, Keynote, Google Slides, Prezi, or Canva. The presenter designs their slides as documents rather than visual aids. That means overloaded slides that double as the pre-read or the handout. As I mentioned earlier, I'm not saying the pre-read is unimportant, it is often essential, but it should be different to your slides.

Documents on a screen don't work as visual aids. Why? Because human beings will either read or listen. It's almost impossible to do both. Too much text overloads our cognitive systems as we try to decipher complicated slides. Plus, they encourage you to read the slides to your audience rather than communicate your ideas to them.

We are the problem

PowerPoint presentations have become a cultural norm within organisations. When did you last attend a presentation that didn't have some sort of PowerPoint attached? It's perplexing to consider what we did thirty-five years ago when PowerPoint didn't exist. How on earth did people present? Chalkboards and pointers?

As soon as we hear we'll be doing a presentation, most of us immediately think 'slides.' We begin constructing our message by heading straight to PowerPoint. The result is a slide deck with no link to any underlying point or intention, as we haven't stopped to consider what our objective is and what our messaging needs to be. However, if we begin constructing our slides after we already have our big idea and our core content sorted, slide creation becomes so much easier. We have a much greater chance of creating slides that truly aid the message rather than just repeat it. That's why we've got to Chapter Ten before we discuss slides.

Our slide bias

Consider the way we set up our boardrooms or training rooms. Are they not biased toward displays of slides rather than human connection? Picture a typical boardroom – it's usually a long rectangular table with maybe a dozen chairs around it. And what's in the prime position at the head of the table? It's not the presenter. It's a large screen, usually fixed to a wall, dominating where a presenter should stand and engage their room. What does that tell an audience is important? The presenter or the slides? That's right. The slides. I've seen many situations where the screen position pushes the presenter off to the side and out of audience view.

Consider some of these room setups.

As with most things, visual aid software is not the problem; it's how we use it. (Although many would argue corporate templates that encourage heavy text content, animation effects, auto-content wizards, and clichéd clipart do much to encourage its misuse.) However, we now know that seeing images while hearing narration works brilliantly and greatly increases our ability to retain information.

Vision trumps all the other senses

In his book, *Brain Rules,* Dr John Medina writes that seventy-five per cent of what we know has come to us visually, adding that vision will trump all the other senses. It also turns out that human beings are terrific at remembering pictures. It's called the PSE – or the Picture Superiority Effect. 'If information is presented orally,' Medina writes, 'people remember about ten per cent, tested seventy-two hours after exposure. That figure goes up to sixty-five per cent if you add a picture.'[2]

That doesn't mean all our slides should become pretty pictures. However, we know that text is more complicated for the brain to process, and too much on slides overloads our cognitive systems. As the marketing guru, Seth Godin, notes, 'If all you want to do is create a file of facts and figures, cancel the meeting and send in a report.'[3]

So, what can we do about it? Before you answer that question – decide whether you even need slides in your presentation.

Going commando

Just because you're delivering a presentation doesn't automatically mean you need a slide deck. What if a few diagrams or sketches on a whiteboard would do? There's something engaging about a presenter comfortably sketching out their ideas out as they speak. A whiteboard or flip chart can work brilliantly – especially when part of your presentation may seek to elicit ideas from an audience. It can also be a great credibility builder.

Other options could include talking through a handout, doing a hands-on demonstration, or simply having no visuals at all. Have any of the great speeches of history ever needed PowerPoint slides? Imagine Barack Obama giving his 'Yes we can' address with a twenty slide PowerPoint accompaniment – madness!

PowerPoint has become an addiction to the point that people have often never experienced presenting without it. When you suggest going slide-free, their immediate reaction is panic. But if you've genuinely done your work, it's astonishing how effective you can be.

A few years back, a participant on one of my programmes recounted the experience of attending a large international conference of research scientists at a fancy resort in the mountains of Austria. Early in the morning of the second day, a large storm blew in, bringing down trees and causing a power surge that knocked out the conference facility's AV equipment.

Suddenly, everyone presenting that day had to face doing without using their prepared visual aids. What happened next was fascinating. People had to communicate their ideas – often creatively – and that freed them up to engage. Some used whiteboards, while others split the audience into groups to workshop ideas, and others just talked. The audience loved it. It was a wonderful outcome from what could have been a disaster. In fact, my participant noted it was the most engaging conference he'd ever attended, and the conference organisers agreed to follow a similar minimal-slide model for all future conferences.

Designing great slides

If you really do want to use slides, then here are eight principles to keep in mind as you create your slide deck.

1. *Make your handouts or pre-reads different*

If you're using the slides as a pre-read or handout, you're not presenting a visual aid; you're presenting a document. I suggest you create two pieces of collateral. The first is your pre-read (or handout) that has all the detail required for the audience to absorb in their own time. Second are your simple, elegant slides highlighting your key points and visually reinforcing you as the presenter. Putting all the supporting details in a handout saves you from feeling like you must cram all the information onto your slides. Yes, I know this will take a little more time, but simply copying and pasting all your spreadsheets, or graphs, or figures onto slides without considering your audience is ineffective and a recipe for cognitive overload and boredom.

2. *Create slides that reinforce your message, not repeat it*

I first heard this idea from marketing guru Seth Godin, and it's brilliant. Rather than building slides that act as a teleprompter to keep you on track, think instead about how to engage your audience with simple visuals that reinforce your ideas.[4] Naturally, images work well for this – but so do just a few key words or diagrams. One trick I have clients do is count the number of words on each of their slides. More than fifty words? Then it should probably be a document, not a visual aid. Fewer than forty words and we're starting to get better.

Simplicity is key. Of course, having simple slides means you must fill in the gaps for the audience with your engaging delivery.

It's critical that you know your stuff so you can effortlessly communicate the core concepts of each slide. Yes, that will take you a little more time (and practise), but your audience will thank you for it. You'll also find access to a few simple notes will help keep you on track.

'Ok, that's all well and good,' I hear you say, 'but what if I present a lot of data or numbers?'

That brings me to the next principle.

3. *Highlight meaning*

Slide guru Nancy Duarte has wise advice in her seminal book on slide creation, *Slide:ology*.[5] She writes that it's not so much the data that's important, but rather the meaning of that data to an audience. That means you should ensure you *highlight the meaning* as you present your slides. This could be as simple as animating a circle to appear around a key dataset or changing the colour of a bar in a chart. It also means making sure your charts or data are decipherable.

Remember, as you're building your deck, you're close to your screen, and everything will be readable to you. Take a moment to step backwards and see if you can still see what's on your slide. If your audience can't read the detail – it's pointless as a visual aid.

It shouldn't take any longer than three seconds for the audience to comprehend your slides. Duarte calls this the 'glance test' and suggests thinking of your slide like a billboard. A quick glance, and you comprehend the meaning.[6] You can make that comprehension easier by talking them through the key focus areas. Don't be afraid to walk up to your screen and point directly to where you'd like them to look. Only don't have your back to them for too long, of course.

4. Bullets kill

Too many bullets will kill your presentation so try to use them sparingly. Otherwise, it's easy to get caught up in a teleprompting 'read-off-the-screen' style. If you insist on their use, try to follow these rules:

- **1-5-5:** One idea per slide, five lines per slide, five words per line.

- **Write in headlines:** you don't need to write full sentences on your slides.

- **Animate bullets to appear on click:** When you animate bullets and bring them up one point at a time, you're controlling the flow of information. You can then talk to each point, one at a time, without the audience reading on and getting ahead of your ideas.

- **Use large, simple fonts.** Small fonts in documents are fine. However, any font size smaller than 18 point will seem small when on a slide, and your audience may have difficulty reading it. Think 24+ for all your fonts, and you'll be safe.

5. Use good quality images

One of the best resources for a great presentation is access to quality images. If your organisation is serious about the quality of their presentations, then they should have an image bank available to you. Another option is to source your images from a good stock photography website. Unsplash.com is free and has wonderful images for download. An advanced Google image search will give you the option to source images from the web that are free to use and unencumbered by copyright. Try your best to avoid cliched images or ClipArt. And watch your file size and aspect ratio. An image that is too small or stretched out of proportion will end up looking blurry and unprofessional. Think like a designer. Make sure you're arranging your slide content with elegance and simplicity.

6. *Avoid fancy effects and transitions*

Unless you really know what you're doing, avoid cheesy effects, animations and transitions. All they do is weaken your content and distract your audience. I've seen many a presentation stalled by animations or transitions that take too long to execute. The presenter's first instinct is to think their slide's not advancing properly. Next minute, you'll be three slides ahead of where you need to be as, in panic, you've mistakenly clicked on too far.

7. *Create a narrative with top-line sentences*

Another terrific technique, particularly for data-heavy presentations, is to create a top-line sentence that shares the core insight or idea of each slide. You can then look at the Slide Sorter view in PowerPoint, which enables you to see all your slides in a storyboard format. If you read the top line sentence of each slide consecutively, they should form a coherent narrative for your audience.

8. *Make the most of your title slide*

My work colleague calls the title slide 'great real estate that is often neglected.' Imagine a title slide that reads *Q3 Marketing Update*. Yawn. Your title slide will be the first that people will see and will likely be up on the screen for a good deal of time while people arrive. So, why not make it compelling? Try taking something in your big idea or from your obstacles (from Chapter Six) to use as inspiration for your title slides. What if *'Q3 Marketing Update'* became *'Customer sentiment is softening – should we be worried?'*

Presenter secrets

The 'B' key

This is a handy little trick that blacks out the screen and encourages the audience to engage with you. If you notice your audience gazing intently at your screen and you want their attention back, press the 'B' key. I guarantee all eyes will immediately be on you. Sometimes I'll use this option when I'm telling a story or answering a detailed question.

Use presenter view

Presenter view in PowerPoint enables you to see the slide you're currently showing, the slide that's coming next, and your notes – all at once. I highly recommend using this tool. Seeing the slide approaching before your audience means you can transition much more effectively from one to the next.

Typically, when people are presenting with slides, the process is: click to advance, cue their idea from the slide, then speak that idea to an audience. When you use presenter view, you can invert that process. First, cue your idea by observing the slide that's coming next, then click to advance to that slide as you begin speaking to it. It might take a few practices to master, but you will look super slick and professional if you nail it.

Get a clicker

A remote slide-advancer is an essential tool for any regular presenter. It gives you the ability to use all the space available as you don't have to constantly return to your computer to advance your slides. Be sure to use a reputable brand with a good range and battery life, and avoid phone-based or Bluetooth systems.

There you have it. Eight simple principles, plus three little tricks, to ensure the slides you create are enhancing your message rather than detracting from it. Now that your messaging is complete let's dig into your delivery.

Quick Tips: *Visual Aids*

- Visual aids are for your audience, not a script to keep you on track.
- Avoid presenting to documents – your slides should be different to your pre-read or handout.
- Keep your slides elegant and simple – think like a designer.
- Create slides that reinforce your message, not just repeat it.
- Keep your bullets to 1-5-5. One idea per slide, maximum five bullets per slide, maximum five words per bullet.
- Use large fonts.

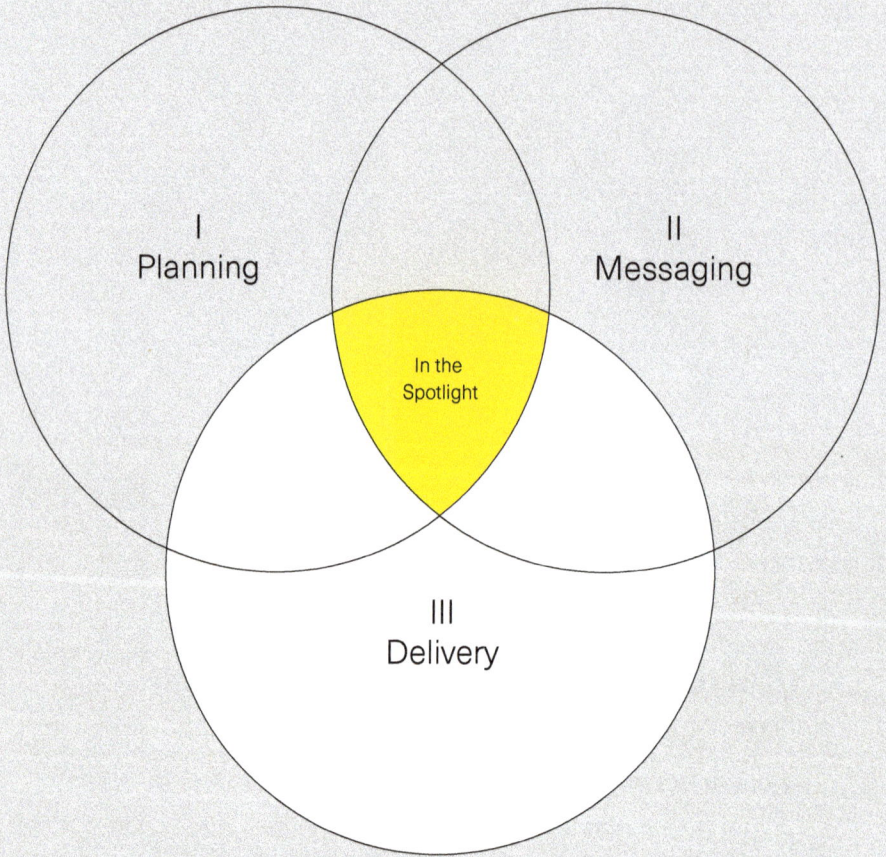

I
Planning

II
Messaging

In the
Spotlight

III
Delivery

Section III
Delivery

Chapter Ten

Practise

Warning: Don't skip this chapter!

Rehearsing your presentation out loud is a vitally important step toward the spotlight. From actors to athletes, musicians to magicians, practising is fundamental to success. The same is true for presenters. Rehearsing will always, yes, always, lead to a better presentation.

In my experience, every time you practise out loud, your presentation will improve by twenty per cent (for the first three times). It is also the single most effective way to manage your speaking nerves. But most people don't practise at all – or when they do, they don't practise effectively or efficiently.

A few years ago, I did an informal survey asking how and where people practised their presentations. The most common responses? Sitting quietly by themselves, in the shower, or in the car on the way to work. Nowhere near ideal, but better than nothing at all.

Practise makes perfect sense

Good practise means putting yourself into an environment that mostly mirrors the actual setting in which you'll be delivering, then speaking your presentation out loud. That's why actors preparing for a play move their last week of rehearsals into the theatre they'll be performing in. Your brain needs to adapt to your material, the setting and the technology.

Unfamiliarity with the environment creates uncertainty. Uncertainty creates a disconnection with your audience as you try to make sense of the room, the distance between you and your audience, the technology, and whatever else you may need to negotiate – all while trying to communicate your ideas. The magic happens when you are at ease with your content and the environment, and free to focus on your audience. Simply put, the more you practise, the freer you are to connect.

Here are some tips to make the most of your practise.

Find a good room

If you can manage it, the first choice for your practise space should be the room you'll be presenting in. See if you can get access, maybe early in the morning or after-hours. Perhaps an internal booking system will allow you to reserve it. Your next best option is a similar-sized space with similar tech capability. Failing that, any quiet room that enables you to focus, speak with your full voice and not feel self-conscious will do. You can even plug your computer into the back of your living room TV, and practise to your cat. Better than nothing, right?

Practise with your tech

Set up your practise space as closely as possible to how it will be on the day. That may mean moving a few chairs or tables around. Work out where your audience will be and where you'll be standing (or sitting). If you're using slides and a clicker, get those all plugged in and ready to go. Try to position yourself in the middle of the stage/presentation area with the projection screen to the side and slightly behind you. Refer to page 127 and 129 for some examples.

Remember, you are the most important thing, so you should be centre stage. Often that is difficult as the corporate default position for projection screens is smack bang in the middle – which inevitably forces the presenter to the sides of the room. Place your laptop in front of you where you can glance at it and back to the audience without having to move or turn away. This will be better than looking behind you. Test your clicker and slides are working before you begin. If you're using video or sound, test that too. Beware of just accepting things the way they are. For example, if you need to move some tables around to get yourself and your audience in a better position – do it. If your HDMI cable's too short, find a longer one. Be pro-active in getting yourself sorted.

Stand up

Once your audience numbers more than six to eight, you will be more effective if you stand. So make sure to practise doing so. If you practise while standing, then find it's better to sit during the presentation – you'll still be fine. Practising while sitting and then finding you need to stand is much more challenging. Better to be safe than sorry. (And yes, I know practising while standing is harder, and you may feel more awkward. But you will develop your presentation skills much faster by doing so.)

Aim for three run-throughs – out loud

Out loud means at the volume you mean to be on the day. Three times is realistically achievable for most people. If you want to do more, go for it, but beware of obsessing or over-practising. Remember, it's just a presentation, and you might want to stagger your rehearsals over a few days.

I can almost guarantee that you'll find moments in your presentation that aren't working well the first time through, so be sure to iterate and fine-tune your presentation as you go along. Don't be tempted to start adding more and more information. At this point, you should be refining.

Don't memorise; keep it conversational

There's no need to remember your presentation word-for-word. Rather, think of talking naturally to a series of points. And watch out for 'presenter voice'. I often hear people's natural voices become stiff and formal as soon as they begin presenting. Suddenly, they seem to lose their authenticity and sound like they're back in high school giving a speech rather than delivering a presentation in an organisation. This usually happens when they've tried to memorise their presentation.

Keep it conversational, warm and friendly. And don't worry if it comes out a little different every time you practise. If you're still communicating your important ideas, that's completely fine. Remember, when it comes time to deliver, your audience will be hearing this for the first time. They will have no clue it was completely different in your last rehearsal.

Create notes if you need them

The trick with notes is to have them somewhere you can glance at them to keep you (or get you back) on track. As described in the last chapter, use Presenter view mode in PowerPoint to store your notes for each slide. You can then see them on your computer screen as you're presenting. The default space and text for your notes is fairly small, so use a big font and keep them simple.

Another option is to print your slides in notes layout. This will give you a hard copy of the slides with your notes at the bottom. These can be a bit cumbersome, so I suggest putting them in a ring binder open in front of you, so you can easily turn each page as you progress.

You can also handwrite or type your notes into our structure template downloadable from www.thepickeringgroup.com/stepintothespotlight. Place this on a table in front of you as you practise. Remember, notes are there to keep you on track with key points, not to be read as a script. Watch out for holding loose sheets of paper – especially if you're a shaker. And avoid using cue cards – we're not at a high-school speech competition.

Time your presentation

Nobody likes presentations that go over time. It's disrespectful, so be sure you've timed your presentation to allow any expected interaction and a Q&A. As I mentioned in Chapter Four, if you have a thirty-minute slot, aim to make your presentation twenty minutes. If you finish early, that's great. Everyone wants more time.

Practise your presentation in chunks

Sometimes this is more effective than practising the whole presentation at once. Adjust and iterate as you go along. For example, practise your opening, then change anything that's not working and do it again to cement the changes. Repeat this process for the next section, then the next...and so on.

Do a dry run to a mock audience

This is critical for high-stakes or high-status audiences, such as a large pitch. Assemble a group of trusted colleagues to act as your mock audience. Present to them and get them to ask you the tough questions. Receive their feedback and adjust as necessary.

Remember to allow for time to adjust. Completing this step one hour before you present is better than not doing it at all, but it doesn't leave any time to make and practise necessary changes. Be careful not to overwhelm yourself with obsessive last-minute changes. I usually decide twenty-four hours out to make no more changes to content. Just let it be.

Presenting in teams

While it's great that you're not up there alone, more people can add complications if not managed well. If you find yourself presenting as a team, keep the following in mind.

If you're presenting as a team, prepare as a team

Beware of preparing in isolation and then trying to mash it together at the last minute. It won't work well. The first step should be working through your presentation canvas together and agreeing on Point A and Point B. From here, people can individually begin to assemble the content they're responsible for. Nominate someone to take the lead, construct the opening and pull the content into a coherent narrative. Make sure your slides have a cohesive design feel. Come back together to practise.

Don't have too many speakers

A presentation can get very clunky if there are more than three speakers. While a change of speaker can be great for audience engagement, momentum is the key. Don't let the presentation lag when you change. Have each speaker include a transition statement to the next: 'I'm now going to hand you over to Jessie, who will break down the financial analysis in more detail...'

Sort your transitions and logistics

Plan where you'll have the other speakers placed and waiting during the presentation. Practise getting them to and from their spots. Decide how you'll transfer the clicker and mics. Beware of having them stand nervously on-stage behind you; it risks drawing unwanted attention. If all the speakers are sharing the stage, those waiting to speak should focus their attention on the presenter, not stare at the floor or their notes. Have them smile at the presenter's jokes, or nod in agreement when they say something important.

Allow more time to practise material that's not yours

It's more challenging to present ideas, information and slides that someone else has created. If you find you must, make sure you've allowed more time for practise. You will need to work more on getting the presentation to a point where you can own it and not have to read the slides.

Handling questions

Self-confident people aren't afraid to have their views challenged. They relish the intellectual combat that enriches ideas. – Jack Welch

Questions are good so embrace them. Answering them clearly and confidently is almost as important as the presentation itself. Never underestimate the importance of nailing the Q&A. The credibility of your answers may well make or break the entire presentation. Answer them well, and you will inspire confidence and commitment from your audience. Preparing for them is the key to success. If you're getting questions, it means your audience is engaged with your ideas. An absence of any questions could well be a bad sign.

Preparing for questions

Anticipate

You need to think hard about the questions that will likely come your way. Strategise around how to answer them. Ask trusted colleagues with relevant expertise to listen to your presentation and help you anticipate any questions that may follow. Pro tip: The audience obstacles you defined when crafting your Point B in Chapter Five will give you clues about the questions you may get.

Set expectations upfront and manage them well

Let the audience know what you expect of them. For example, you could say, 'Feel free to ask questions as we go,' or 'Because we're pushed for time, I'd ask you to hold questions till the end.'

In most business presentations, audiences expect to ask questions as you go along – especially with high-status groups like senior leadership teams. This can keep the flow conversational and engaging. However, the risk is keeping to time and not letting strong personalities derail your presentation. You'll need to stay assertive in keeping on track. For large groups or hostile audiences, hold questions until the end and have an independent moderator to help with crowd control.

Responding to questions

Listen very carefully

Respect the questioner, even if it's a ridiculous or stupid question. Don't react negatively, such as rolling your eyes. Look at them. Be attentive. Nod as they're speaking. Don't anticipate the question or cut them off. Let them finish. Your job is to win them over, not insult or embarrass them.

Repeat the question

This validates the person asking the question and helps you understand it. It also helps other people in the room hear what the question was and gives you time to formulate your answer.

Give yourself time to think

There's no need to rush into an answer. Take time, within reason, to compose your thoughts.

That's a great question!

Avoid this phrase. It can seem insincere and sends the message that every other question asked was anything but great.

What if I don't know the answer?

Use these four Ds to help:

Deal with it and tell the truth – with caveats if need be. If you don't know the answer to something, don't just make it up. Firstly, it's unethical. Secondly, if you get it wrong and the audience knows it, it will destroy your credibility. If you are unsure of the precise answer, you can add a caveat. For example: 'My current understanding of the situation is...' or 'I believe it's around...'

Delay. 'My apologies, I don't have the answer to that right now. Let me come back to you with those details.'

Defer to someone with expertise. 'Nick, you're probably best suited to answer that question.' Just be sure Nick is ready for it, and you're not throwing him under the proverbial bus.

Deploy. If you don't yet have the full details (or can't reveal them), deploy a tactic that politicians frequently use: 'I'm sorry I can't answer that right now, but what I *can* say is...'.

Quick Tips: *Practise*

• Don't skip your practise. It will *always* lead to a better
  presentation.

• As a rule of thumb, aim to practise your presentation three
  times out loud – but once is better than not at all.

• See if you can practise where you'll be presenting or in a similar
  room. Practise with your technology, and try standing up.

• For high-stakes presentations or pitches, do a dry run with
  a mock audience.

• Questions are good. Prepare for them. Anticipate what you'll
  be asked and practise how you'll respond.

Chapter Eleven

Courage

Courage is resistance to fear, mastery of fear, not absence of fear.
– Mark Twain

Can we pause for a moment here and think about how far you've come. Amazing. You're now just moments away from stepping into the spotlight and delighting your audience with a fantastic presentation. Are your nerves still causing some issues? This chapter's got you covered.

Let's talk about anxiety

A few years back, I was chatting with a psychologist friend about techniques to manage speaking nerves. She shared a definition of anxiety that has stuck with me since. 'Anxiety comes from an over-estimation of a problem or issue, coupled with an under-estimation of your ability to deal or cope with it.'

I love this definition and have used it often with coaching clients over the years. It asks us to seek perspective on the challenge ahead – in this case, a looming presentation. What are our thoughts about it? What is the narrative we're telling ourselves? Are we catastrophising?

The definition also encourages us to back ourselves and ask whether our perception of our ability to deliver effectively aligns with reality.

The limping wildebeest

Why does speaking – one of the most ordinary and natural things most of us do daily with complete ease – become so complicated in front of an audience? The simple answer is fear: fear of humiliation; fear of being judged not good enough; fear of being expunged from the safety and anonymity of the group and left alone to be devoured by hungry lions.

When you present, you are exposed and noticed. At a primal level, to be seen is to be a target. Our bodies produce adrenaline and cortisol to deal with the perceived threat. This reaction is called the 'fight or flight' syndrome, and it hinders our ability to stay connected with our audience.

Notice how this aligns with Rodenburg's three circles that we discussed in Chapter Two? Uncontrolled fight or flight is a major reason we become trapped in our shadow archetypes. As author and presentation expert Jerry Weissman writes, 'adrenaline is the cause, fight or flight is the effect, and the result is either defensive or anxious behaviour.'[1]

The consequences of presenting anxiety

When we have an anxiety overload while presenting, all sorts of strange things begin to happen both physically and vocally. Maybe these nerves will manifest as mind-blanks, shaking, sweating, speaking too fast, filled pauses (ums and ahs), stumbling over words, lack of eye contact and a general difficulty connecting with an audience. The physical (body language) and vocal (vocal variety) sub-conscious messages can contradict our presentation objective.

For better or for worse, your audience will pick up the signals you are sending.

So, what can we do about it?

Think manage, not banish

Let's take a moment right here to reframe how you might think about nerves. Often presenters regard them as something to conquer – as though they're a foreign invader out to destroy us. I don't think this mindset is particularly helpful, and I've never met anyone who has been entirely successful in eliminating their speaking nerves. Instead, let's accept that nerves come with the territory and manage them, so they're working for us, not against us. Think of anxiety as a spectrum, from panic at one end and nerve-free at the other. You want to have a few manageable butterflies. A little bit is a good thing; it will energise and focus you – and show you care.

Don't obsess over trying to be confident

Confidence is a feeling. When it comes to presenting, there are two types: the confidence you feel in yourself and the confidence your audience feels in you. Your first duty is to the latter. Your job as a presenter is to get your audience to have confidence in you and your ideas. If you do that successfully, they are far more likely to be persuaded and engaged. Yes, confidence in yourself matters, but here's the thing, your audience are not mind-readers. They will not know you are super nervous unless you give it away.

Similarly, if you have complete confidence in yourself but fail to get the confidence of the audience, you risk coming across as arrogant or indifferent. Remember, the confidence of the room is yours to lose. So don't obsess over trying to be more confident. Instead, focus on being courageous.

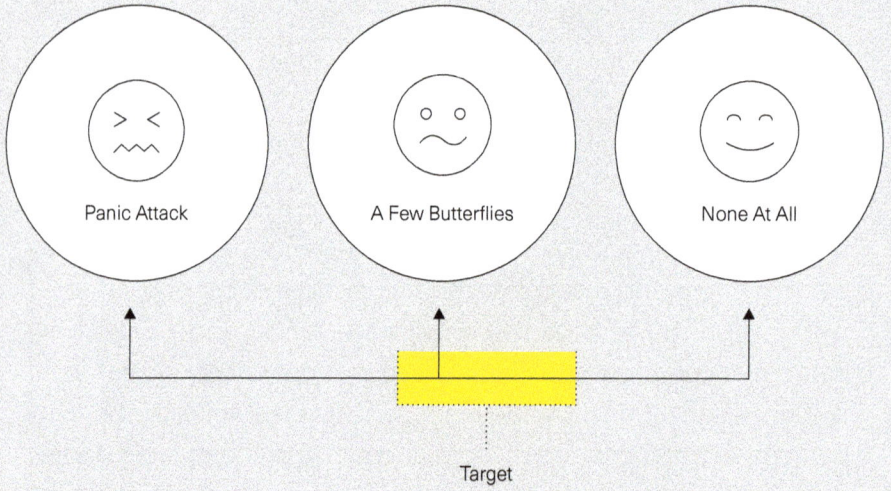

Figure 26: Anxiety as a spectrum

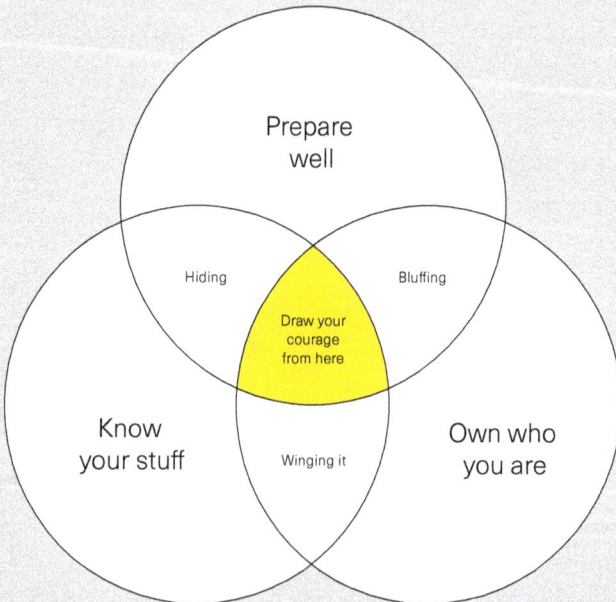

Figure 27: The courage model

Amplify your courage

Courage trumps confidence. If confidence is the light your audience sees shining from you, then courage is the energy that powers that light. You can't deny courage its place. It is fierce and illuminating. Everyone has it, but some find it harder to access than others. When it comes to presenting, you can find your courage with the following three amplifiers.

1. Know your stuff. This is up to you.

2. Prepare well. That's what this book is all about.

3. Own who you are. Get comfortable in your own skin.

The stronger you are in each of these, the more courage you will have to draw from. You need all three amplifiers working for you. Notice where the circles intersect the courage model (figure 27). If you *know your stuff* and *own who you are* but you're not *preparing well*, you're *winging it*. If you *prepare well* and *own who you are* but don't *know your stuff*, you're *bluffing*. If you *prepare well* and *know your stuff* but don't *own who you are*, you're *hiding*.

One of my favourite exercises on the second day of my two-day presentation skills programmes is to have participants create a 'Mini TED Talk.' Using the process outlined in this book, they have two hours to prepare from scratch (including time for practise), a six-minute presentation on a topic they feel strongly about.

When I first started doing this exercise, I noticed something remarkable. Participants who came into the programme with high anxiety and self-conscious delivery habits became more comfortable and authentic. They brought more conviction to their ideas. They inspired more confidence in their audience – were more grounded in their delivery. What's more, they would notice that change in themselves – and be excited by it.

I realised these were the courage amplifiers doing their work. Sure, they'd been introduced to a process that enabled them to prepare well in a short time, but it wasn't just about the prep. Their brief was to create a presentation on a topic they felt strongly about. As such, participants would most often choose subjects they were highly knowledgeable about – even if that subject was as simple as baking the perfect scone (which, as it turns out, is not that simple).

This surety of knowledge gave them courage and conviction. Add to that the permission to be themselves, and I would see, time and again, people stepping quickly and confidently out of the shadows and into the spotlight. So let me say it again. Know your stuff. Prepare well. Own who you are.

Do you notice anything about these courage amplifiers? They are the opposite of the three shadow keepers from Chapter One. These three amplifiers will help propel you into the spotlight.

Managing your nerves

There is nothing either good or bad, but thinking makes it so.

– William Shakespeare (Hamlet)

The next part of this chapter is a compilation of every evidence-based tactic or tool I've encountered that will help you manage your nerves and inspire confidence. However, every suggestion assumes you are taking the time to prepare well. That means following the process outlined in this book. That will always be the single biggest thing you can do to manage your nerves – there are no shortcuts. Avoid procrastinating and start preparing early. If you are poorly prepared and the presentation doesn't go well, you will only reinforce your anxiety and trap yourself in the shadows. You may notice a couple of the following suggestions we've already touched on. I've purposely chosen to mention them again here so there's one comprehensive section in this book you can visit that covers all our anxiety-reducing tips. That sections starts right here. (You can also download these tips on a printable A3 cheat sheet from www.thepickeringgroup.com/stepintothespotlight)

In the weeks leading up to your presentation:

Care about your topic

If you can, present on a topic you care deeply about – or find a way to care about the topic you're presenting. I accept that for many presentations, that's easier said than done. However, having (or finding) a real need to communicate will shift the focus away from yourself and on to the people who will benefit from the information you have to share.

Practise self-awareness

Become aware of your mental models and self-sabotaging behaviours, and remember that feelings are not facts. Evidence shows that being mindful and accepting your feelings around presenting (both good and bad) can help reduce your anxiety.[2]

You don't need to obsess about turning negative thoughts into positive; just accept and note them. Remember, anxiety is about the future. You may be worried about what you think might happen and what you think your audience will think of you. But you're not a fortune-teller or a mind-reader, so find your present self. And further to that point…

Engage in meditation and mindfulness

It works. The growing body of evidence around the efficacy of regular mindfulness practise in reducing general anxiety is hard to ignore.[3]

Calm and Headspace are terrific apps to begin an exploration into mindfulness and meditation.

In the days leading:

Practise, practise, practise – it's fundamental!

It's so fundamental that we're reinforcing it again in this chapter. Remember, for new material, aim to practise at least three times out loud – with your full voice – and standing up. That doesn't include in the shower, in front of the mirror, or in the car on the way to the presentation.

Don't memorise a script

Instead, construct a roadmap for yourself, a series of points to talk to. And keep it conversational and alive. Yes, you need to know your subject very well to do this effectively. If not, your attention will turn inward, away from your audience, as you try to remember what you need to say.

Practise with a mock audience

Assemble a group of friends or colleagues and present to them. Ask for constructive feedback and make sure you've allowed time to implement their suggestions. Rehearse in the actual space if you can. Don't leave too long a gap between sessions. The more your presentation subject is embedded in your mind, the more you will be free to connect with your audience.

The day before:

Do a dry run

If you can, do a final practise in the actual room or space you'll be in. Practise with all your technology. Make sure it's working and that you have backups. Double-check for errors in your slides, then stop making last-minute changes to your presentation. Leave it alone.

Plan travel logistics

If you're presenting off-site, work out the logistics, such as travel time and parking arrangements. Arrive early. Allow for a contingency. There's nothing worse than feeling rushed. If you're flying or out of the country, this should happen a lot earlier.

Plan what you're going to wear

Dress appropriately for the encounter and wear something that makes you feel a million bucks. Avoid noisy or distracting jewellery. Get your hair done (no radical changes or trying a new stylist!) or get a massage. Practise a bit of self-compassion. You deserve it.

Stick to your routine

Get a good night's sleep, and avoid having the celebratory wine too early.

The morning of:

Review

Look over your notes and your slide deck. Double-check that any embedded media is working. Reconnect with your presentation objective.

Exercise

Moderate cardio exercise on the day of presenting releases endorphins and mitigates the effect of adrenaline and cortisol.[4] But don't go too crazy – especially if you don't usually exercise.

Apply sweat-blocking deodorant

If you're a heavy perspirer, you can get special sweat-blocking deodorant from a pharmacy. It's quite thick, but it helps to avoid sweat circles.

Don't try to calm down

It's totally ok to be nervous. Trying to calm down doesn't work. Research noted by psychologist Adam Grant showed that trying to calm yourself resulted in a poorer performance when giving a public speech.[5]

Convert your nerves into excitement

Instead of saying 'I am calm,' try 'I am excited.' You want to have your fire a bit stoked – but stay focused and grounded. Grant adds, 'Anxiety is an intense emotion, and it's hard to make it vanish quickly in the face of uncertainty. It's easier to convert anxiety into another strong emotion like excitement.'[6]

Check and arrange the space

If you can, familiarise yourself with your presentation space. Check that the technology is working. Get a feel for the room and, if possible, arrange it to work for you. Have your computer as a comfort monitor in front of you. Make room for your notes. Imagine yourself succeeding in the space.

Avoid too much caffeine

Stick to your normal amount for a day, but pull back right before your presentation. It can make you jittery.

Just before:

Double-check your tech

Make sure your technology is set up and working properly. Check that any embedded media plays and the sound is working.

Review

Go over your objective and your opening.

Find your 'state of readiness'

If you watch great athletes and actors, their preparation always starts in a state of readiness. Here's how you find it: Arms released at the sides. Feet hip-width apart and slightly out. Weight balanced between right and left, and ever-so-slightly forward on the balls of the feet. Knees not locked. Shoulders relaxed. Head floating and relaxed on the shoulders. Jaw released, not clenched. This is the most open position we can be in physically, although at first, it might feel unnatural and vulnerable. Persevere – practise – and it will soon feel natural. And remember, the audience thinks you look relaxed, connected and open.

Breathe

Centre yourself. Try this exercise to ground yourself. Breathe in on a three count, hold for a four count – breathe out on a five count. Repeat the sequence ten times.

Draw on your courage

Be ambitious for yourself. Presenting takes guts.

During:

Play it cool

Don't tell your audience that you're nervous, and don't apologise for your nerves. Release yourself from the pressure of having to be perfect.

Remember to keep it conversational

Most business audiences don't want to hear a memorised robot script. They want to see someone speaking with conviction, but naturally from the heart. And the audience doesn't know how the presentation is supposed to be. It's totally fine if it's a little different to how you practised.

Connect with your audience, and let it all go

Respect your audience. After all, they are the sole reason you are there. Focus on their needs. You are there to be of service to them, not to obsess over your own self-regard. Focus on connecting your ideas to them and understand what you want them to feel – this will drive your delivery.

'To reduce the fear of public speaking,' says Jerry Weissman, 'you must shift your focus away from your concerns about your own success or failure and think about whether each and every individual in every audience is getting the message of your pitch.'[7] It's astounding what a difference this shift in focus can make. Weismann adds, 'When you connect with your audience and sense their responsiveness, your adrenaline and stress recede. When the audience observes a speaker's ease and confidence, they too experience a feeling of confidence and are more receptive to the speaker's message.'

Read the room

Notice eye-contact and head-nods. These will calm you and let you know you're on the right track. These are the end-game for a business presentation. If your audience is nodding at you, it's very unlikely they're disagreeing with your idea.

Watch the time

Be aware of the time and what your audience may need. Maybe it's time for a break or a discussion. Adjust if you need one too. Check in with them. Finish on time.

After:

Reflect

Find quiet time to process and reflect – especially if you're an introvert.

Acknowledge your achievement

No point in obsessing over your slip-ups – we all make them.

Follow-up

Promptly follow-up by emailing a thank you, action points or providing any requested information.

Repeat

Seek out another opportunity to present – especially if you're actively working to manage your fear of public speaking. Try not to leave it too long before your next presentation encounter.

Quick Tips: *Courage*

- A bit of presenting anxiety is normal and useful. Focus on managing, not banishing your nerves.

- Courage trumps confidence. Maximise your courage with the three courage amplifiers – know your stuff, prepare well and own who you are.

- The single biggest way to manage your anxiety is to follow the process outlined in this book.

- If you're still super nervous, delve into this chapter and commit to trying every suggestion listed.

Chapter Twelve

Connect

Nor do not saw the air too much with your hand, thus,
but use all gently; for in the very torrent, tempest, and,
as I may say, the whirlwind of passion, you must acquire
and beget a temperance that may give it smoothness…
suit the action to the word, the word to the action.

– William Shakespeare, Hamlet, Act III Scene I

One final task remains. You must now deliver your presentation in a way that connects with your audience's hearts and minds. All the preparation in previous chapters has been designed to lead you to this point. This chapter is in two parts – delivery skills and presenting virtually.

Delivery skills

You should now have at least some awareness of how you come across as a presenter and have started working on practising good delivery habits. In the world of performing arts, this is called developing your craft. It is your ability to naturally use your body and voice to facilitate and enhance the connection between your audience and your idea. Put simply; it's your delivery skills.

Good delivery skills (appropriate eye contact, open body language, and a clear, engaging voice) are like muscles, and they can be trained and strengthened. If you exercise regularly, your fitness improves. If you don't, you get out of shape. The same goes for presenting. That's why if you haven't done a major presentation a while, you may feel a bit rusty and need more practise.

As discussed in Chapter Ten, practising your presentation is crucial for success. During your practise is the best time to be consciously and diligently working on your delivery skills. After all, the best way to get better at presenting is to do lots of it. And, like any skill, a good coach really helps.

Focus first on feeling

The challenge for many presenters is how to deliver with conviction without losing their authenticity. Many feel they need to be an extrovert or a performer to be effective. But the consequence of this mindset can be a style of presenting that sounds nothing like the rhythms of your natural speech. This happens when too much focus is placed on 'performing' rather than connection.

Rather than worrying about being expressive, think about truly connecting with your audience. If you are clear about what you want them to feel, and connect with a real desire to reach them, expression will naturally occur in your voice and body.

Think for a moment. If a toddler runs into the path of oncoming traffic, you have no problem adding emphasis and changing pitch and pace to warn them of the imminent danger. Likewise, when telling your partner about a hilarious (or horrible) event that happened in your day – your delivery adjusts naturally to what you're saying. Conveying passion, conviction and energy becomes easy. It should be just as natural when we present.

How do you do that? Focusing on what you want your audience to feel – whether urgency, concern, worry, valued, intrigued or excited – will allow you to find true conviction in your message. Remember 'think, feel, do' from Chapter Five? The work you did in identifying your objective – Point B – will help guide you here.

Record yourself

A great way to work on your delivery skills is to record a practise session and watch it back. Take a close look at how you're delivering. Notice what you're doing with your body and your voice. Does your body look restless and closed, or grounded, open and relaxed? Now try delivering in different ways. Try keeping your feet grounded or minimising your 'ums and ahs'. Another option is to find a friend or trusted colleague to be your coach. Have them watch you practise and give feedback on where you can improve.

Training for delivery

The goal of your delivery is to be natural and conversational. That doesn't mean we shouldn't train our delivery skill muscles to be stronger and more flexible. Don't forget that the work on your delivery skill should happen during your practising. Once you're in the moment with your audience, just focus on the connection.

Before we breakdown delivery further, let's examine three quick concepts that will help us keep perspective – the four stages of learning, the J Curve and the comfort-zone paradox.

The four stages of learning

Whenever you start developing a skill, such as driving a car or playing a sport, you progress through these four stages of learning. Working on your delivery skills is similar. Perhaps you had no idea you filled

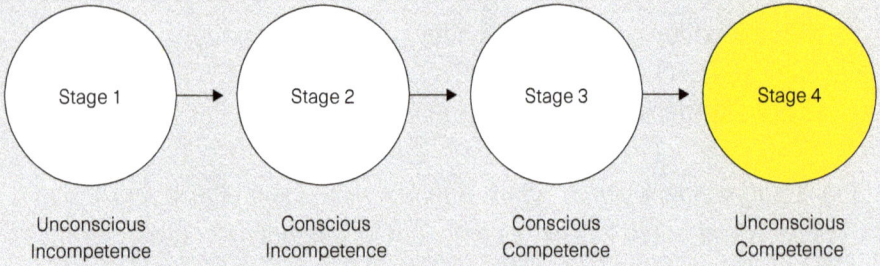

Stage 1 → Stage 2 → Stage 3 → Stage 4

Unconscious
Incompetence

Conscious
Incompetence

Conscious
Competence

Unconscious
Competence

Figure 28: Four stages of learning

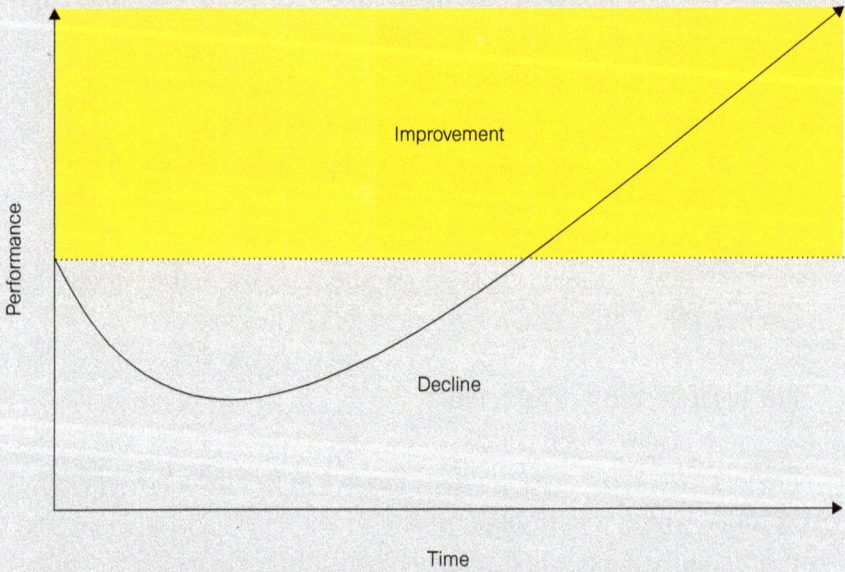

Performance

Improvement

Decline

Time

Figure 29: The J-curve

so many pauses with 'ums and ahs' or that you never look at your audience when talking. That's why recording your practise can be so valuable.

It's important to remember that there is no quick-fire way to becoming better at delivering a presentation. It takes time and a commitment to change. Remember that adage of 'practise makes perfect'? Concentrating on the skill, repeating the skill to cement new habits, and diligence in the regular practise and application of that skill is how you will strengthen your delivery skills muscle.

The J Curve

As you begin your improvement, you may feel you get worse before you get better. This is perfectly normal, and it's called the J-curve. Exploring new techniques at first feels foreign and maybe a little unnatural or clunky. You may become more self-conscious and hyper-aware of everything you could be doing better. Silence your inner-saboteur and persevere. You'll soon pass through that uncomfortable feeling and reach new heights of presentation excellence.

The comfort zone paradox

Jerry Weismann writes about a strange paradox that affects presenters, especially when breaking old presenting habits and learning new ones.[1]

What feels comfortable to you may well look uncomfortable to the audience.

What feels uncomfortable to you may well look comfortable to the audience.

Remember, your feelings are not facts. Developing good presenting habits will undoubtedly make you feel uncomfortable at first as they will put you out of your comfort zone. But persevere, and they will soon feel natural, and you will see improvement.

Breaking down delivery

Delivery can be broken into three important aspects:

Appropriate eye contact

Open body language

A clear, engaging voice

Let's examine each in turn.

Appropriate eye contact

Maintaining eye contact is the most basic of delivery skills and the most powerful. It's powerful because it connects us at a deeply human and personal level. Simply put, in a Western business environment, you need to look at your audience when you're speaking to them. If you don't, they'll form negative opinions about you, even seeing you as dishonest or shady or uncertain.

Sounds basic, right? Here's the catch. Good eye contact is surprisingly difficult to achieve when you don't know your subject matter well enough or if you're excessively nervous. So, make sure you're well-practised, and that you know your material like the back of your hand. A virtual environment makes eye-contact even more challenging, but more on that shortly.

Here are a few tips for good eye contact.

Avoid the skim

When you're nervous, you may tend to give your audience a series of cursory glances. Avoid this. Really work on connecting with them. But don't linger too long – that can also be uncomfortable. Aim for two to three seconds before moving on.

Work the room

Make sure you work the whole room – not just the friendly faces or those closest to you. While you'll naturally be drawn to the attentive faces, try not to keep coming back to them too frequently. Don't forget to pay attention to the key stakeholders.

Segment large audiences

When your audience is particularly large, it becomes more challenging to make individual eye-connect. Segment them into specific blocks, and be sure to work every block. Especially the 'cheap seats' – those furthest away from you.

Open body language

Our body speaks a language of its own, so it's vital that what our body is 'saying' aligns with our message. Often, I see presenters' bodies sending a completely different message to what they're speaking. When there is a discrepancy between the words and the body language, it's the body language the audience will pay attention to.

Match it up

Always strive to ensure your body's message is in alignment with your verbal one. After all, your body language and gestures should be natural and connected expressions of your energy. They serve to physically portray your beliefs, your values, and your passion. When not used or repressed, your apparent sincerity and commitment will suffer. Likewise, over-expressive and over-gesticulating speakers can seem forced, unspecific, and even comical. As with eye contact, if you're particularly nervous or unsure of your content, this may begin to manifest physically through your body, with reactions like a closed-off body positioning, wringing or fidgeting hands, pacing, swaying, rocking, and excessive gesturing.

Voice

Breath

Everything starts and ends with a breath. It's the first thing we do when we enter this world and the last thing we do before we leave it. Effective breathing is the first step to a connected, expressive voice. Connected breath using the diaphragm, free of tension and holds, connects your voice to your audience – and it holds their interest.

Nervous, shallow breathing quite literally deprives the voice of oxygen, weakening its range, power and interest. For further information and exercises on breathing and the voice, I recommend two books by Patsy Rodenburg: *The Right to Speak* [2] and *The Second Circle.* [3]

Training the voice

Even though expression in your voice should occur naturally, we can train it to add more flexibility and stamina. Here are some ways to overcome some of the most common vocal issues.

'Ums, ahs and tchs': The biggest vocal issue I see, especially in Kiwi and Australian men, is too many filled pauses - 'ums and ahs.' If this is your issue, then I suggest practising your presentation with a friend or colleague. 'Ums and ahs' usually manifest in transitions between thoughts. Ask your friend to tap the table lightly every time they hear one. At first, you will find this very distracting, but stick with it and focus on filling the transitions with a silence.

Up-gliding: New Zealanders and Australians tend to trail up at the end of a sentence, which makes everything sound...like a question? If you have this habit, practise sending your inflection down at the end of a sentence. The result is greater authority, credibility, and presence.

Speaking too fast/not pausing: The pause is a powerful skill to master. Look through your presentation notes and mark where pauses may be useful. While running it through, practise incorporating pause in your speaking.

Monotonous voice: A monotonous or boring voice is often caused by anxiety, which tightens the vocal folds, shoulders and jaw. Remember the effects of fight or flight? Anxiety can also result in speeding up or waffling. Take a section of your presentation and run it through, varying your pitch as wildly as you can. You'll feel like a bit of a weirdo, but when you return to speaking at your normal pitch, you'll find your voice is naturally more flexible and varied.

Hedging statements: 'I guess', 'Kinda', 'Basically', 'Sort of.' These are all subtle ways we hedge our statements. For example: 'I guess what I want to talk about today is...' Well, do you guess or do you know? Use the same technique as for 'ums and ahs' to help minimise these.

Poor articulation: If you find yourself getting tongue-tied when speaking, practise the following exercise for ten minutes a day, every day for a month. Be diligent and take your time and annunciate clearly. You'll notice the difference.

Articulation Exercises
First....
La la la na na na da da da ta ta ta (5x)
Ga ga ga la la la (5x)
Ga ga ga la la la ba ba ba ta ta ta (5x)
Nah nay nee nor noo (5x then change consonants to b, p, d, r, v, l m)
Tsu, tsor, tsah, tsay, tsue (5x)
Pa ba ma (switch it around 5x)
Then...
Red leather, yellow leather (10x)
Rubber baby buggy bumpers (10x)
Toy boat (10x)
Aluminium linoleum (10x)
All together now...
I am the very model of a modern major general I've information, vegetable, animal and mineral I know the kings of England and I quote the fights historical From Marathon to Waterloo in order categorical (3x)

Figure 30: Articulation exercise

Virtual presenting

Presenting virtually is more challenging – plain and simple.

First, your ability to connect with your audience through typical social cues such as eye contact and body language is lessened. It is far more challenging to read the reaction your audience is having to your ideas.

Second, audiences behave very differently virtually than when they're face-to-face. Imagine delivering a presentation in a room where half your audience is busy sending emails or surfing the internet? It would be difficult to tolerate. Yet, in a virtual environment, that happens all the time.

Nevertheless, the importance of engaging when presenting is all the more important in virtual settings. Just as you need to be respectful of your audience, so too your audience needs to be respectful of you. You have a mutual responsibility to be as present as possible.

The following techniques will help ensure your virtual presentations are as effective as your face-to-face ones.

Consider your virtual mise en scène

Mise en scène is a term used in film, television and theatre that describes everything placed on stage or in front of the camera – including the actors. It's a French term that translates to 'putting on stage'. The term can also be used to describe the overall visual presentation or 'look' of a production.

Mise en scène includes composition or framing, lighting, costumes, and hair and makeup. As it happens, these are also important for your virtual presentations, but we don't give enough consideration to their impact. Done well, a considered approach to your virtual mise en scène will increase your professionalism, credibility and impact. For my definition of virtual mise en scène, I'll also add sound quality into the mix.

Let's reduce it to three key considerations: camera framing, lighting and sound.

Camera framing

First, try getting your webcam or camera at eye level. It's by far the most flattering angle. Having your camera lower accentuates your neck, chin and eye bags – and who wants that! Having it higher makes you look small and diminutive. If you're presenting with a laptop, the simplest solution is to stack it on a pile of books. If you have a standing desk, try presenting standing up.

Camera framing

Lighting

Sound

Figure 31: Virtual mise en scène

And don't forget about your background. An interesting background can add professionalism and personality to your virtual encounters. Ask yourself, what do I want my background to say about me or my organisation? Can I include branding or banners? Can I curate the background and be creative? Anything's more interesting than a boring grey wall. You could even try a green screen if you're adventurous. Keep in mind that virtual backgrounds on platforms like Zoom or Teams can look tacky. They can also be fun and clever so use with caution and only if you really need to hide your life.

Lighting

Face your light source – don't have it behind you. If you're in a room with a window, face the window. If the window's behind you, you'll just become a big silhouette with all your expression obscured. Another option is to purchase a semi-professional lighting system (ring lights or diffused lights), which professional YouTubers use. Done right, these will make you look fantastic and are relatively inexpensive. Having a little bit of make-up powder on hand to reduce your sheen can also work wonders.

Sound

In a virtual presenting environment, good sound is critical. An audience can usually deal with a poor video stream, but poor sound quality is very agitating and frustrating. Make sure your mic setup is working well for you. The built-in mics in laptops or desktops are not great quality, so you may want to consider investing in some good kit.

Generally, the rule of thumb is that the closer the mic is to your mouth, the better the capture. When further away, the sound tends to echo and pick up a lot of peripheral noise. Podcasting type mics or decent quality headsets can be a good option. So too can wireless lapel mics – just be sure to watch the battery level. As a quick low-cost hack, the mic included on wired Apple EarPods is surprisingly clear.

Figure 25: Room setups and positioning

Avoid the hostage situation

Avoid light behind you

Figure 32: Mise en scène examples

Poor eye-contact inhibits connection

Avoid poor framing

Watch out for low camera angles

Looking great

Let's look at some mise en scène examples:

Other tips for virtual connection.

Ask your audience to keep their cameras on. This will really help you feel you're not presenting in a vacuum.

When speaking, try to look at the camera, rather than just at the screen. This helps your audience feel more connected to you as it appears you're looking directly at them.

Make use of the chat feature. This is great if you have a large audience. Tell them how to engage with you. Ask a question and have them respond in the chat.

Try using virtual breakout rooms. Most platforms now include this feature, and they're a great way to create a more intimate discussion around ideas and change the energy.

Virtual polls are another option and work great if you're running webinars or larger sessions.

Keep your presentation shorter. Being attentive for long periods in a virtual environment is just more challenging. You will often compete for your audience's attention with many other distractions, from emails to children. Be sure you're not keeping them any longer than you must.

Quick Tips: *Connect*

- Good delivery skills (appropriate eye contact, open body-language and a clear, engaging voice) are like muscles – they can be trained and strengthened.

- When presenting, focus on what you want your audience to feel. That will drive your delivery in the most wonderfully authentic way.

- Eye contact is crucial in business and organisational scenarios.

- Be sure to consider your virtual mise en scène – appropriate camera framing, good lighting and clear sound.

- Have your camera at eye level and look down the barrel when you can.

- And finally, trust you've done the work and let it all go. Be of service. Connect your ideas to your audience. Be present.

Afterword

You've done the work, now let it go

Congratulations. You have prepared, and you are ready. You've done the work, so now it's time to let it go and step into the spotlight. At this point, you don't want to be obsessing over your content or worrying about your voice, body language or gestures. That should have happened in your practise.

Now your sole focus should be on us, your audience. You are here to be of service, not to worry about your success or failure. Find joy in your presenting. Take comfort in the idea that you are part of the grand tradition of oratory that has existed for thousands of years. And remember, we need your great ideas to guide us, educate, motivate and inspire us.

Focus on connecting and understanding what you want us to feel. This will drive your delivery and make it come alive in the most natural and engaging ways. Here – in this space of human connection, fully present, with your ideas igniting the imagination of your audience – is where you will be at your most persuasive and inspiring. Welcome to the spotlight.

Where to from here?

My challenge to you now is to be proactive in your pursuit of opportunities to present. In short, say yes. Put yourself out there. If you get asked to present on something, do it. Challenge yourself. Any opportunity is a chance to develop your skills further. The more you do it, the better you'll become and the less anxious you'll be. And reach out for more help if you need it.

At The Pickering Group we offer a range of different programmes to support your development as a presenter and to prepare you for big opportunities. If you'd like to find out more, request an info pack at info@thepickeringgroup.com.

About the Author

Russell Pickering is one of New Zealand's leading specialists in presentation skills and business storytelling. Before founding The Pickering Group, Russell ran Auckland-based communication skills consultancy SpeakEasy and established himself as an expert trainer, facilitator and coach in the field of business communication skills development. He has helped thousands of people, in some of New Zealand and Australia's most visible organisations, become more confident and compelling communicators. His recent clients include PwC, Mercury, Fonterra, Pernod Ricard, Coca-Cola Europacific Partners, Dentsu, Xero, DLA Piper, Livestock Improvement Corporation, Ministry of Foreign Affairs and Trade, and Waka Kotahi.

Russell thrives in the dynamic intersection of the arts and commerce. Originally trained as a professional actor and director, Russell was awarded a Bob Hope Scholarship to study a Master of Fine Arts in Acting at Meadows School of the Arts (SMU) in the United States. As an actor he has appeared in commercial television, feature film, and on regional theatre stages throughout the US and NZ.

More recently, Russell completed his MBA as part of The University of Auckland's Executive programme.

Born and raised in the Waitomo district, he now lives in Auckland with his partner.

www.thepickeringgroup.com

info@thepickeringgroup.com

Endnotes

Introduction

1. Chamorro-Premuzic, T., 2020. *How to Spot an Incompetent Leader*. [Online] Available at: https://hbr.org/2020/03/how-to-spot-an-incompetent-leader [Accessed 7 September 2021].

2. Dweck, C., 2007. *Mindset: The New Psychology of Success*. New York: Ballantine Books.

3. Marks, S. M. &. J., 2019. *Messengers: Who We Listen To, Who We Don't, and Why*. London: Random House Books.

4. Gallo, C., 2019. *The Art of Persuasion Hasn't Changed in 2,000 Years*. [Online] Available at: https://hbr.org/2019/07/the-art-of-persuasion-hasnt-changed-in-2000-years [Accessed 7 September 2021].

5. Nuys, A. V., 2019. *New LinkedIn Research: Upskill Your Employees with the Skills Companies Need Most in 2020*. [Online] Available at: https://www.linkedin.com/business/learning/blog/learning-and-development/most-in-demand-skills-2020 [Accessed 7 September 2021].

6. Duarte, N., 2019. *Data Story: Explain data and inspire action through story*. Oakton, VA: IdeaPress Publishing.

7. Gallo, C., 2019. *The Art of Persuasion Hasn't Changed in 2,000 Years*. [Online] Available at: https://hbr.org/2019/07/the-art-of-persuasion-hasnt-changed-in-2000-years [Accessed 7 September 2021].

CHAPTER ONE: The Trouble with Speaking

1. Chamorro-Premuzic, T., 2014. *Confidence: the surprising truth about how much you need and how to get it.* London: Profile Books.

2. Carnegie, D., 2010. *How To Win Friends And Influence People.* New York: Simon & Schuster.

3. Bersin, J., 2017. *Catch the wave: the 21st-century career.* [Online] Available at: https://www2.deloitte.com/us/en/insights/deloitte-review/issue-21/changing-nature-of-careers-in-21st-century.html

4. Duarte, N., 2019. *Data Story: Explain data and inspire action through story.* Oakton, VA: IdeaPress Publishing.

CHAPTER TWO:
The Archetypes of Organisational Speakers

1. Rodenburg, P., 2008. *The Second Circle.* New York: W. W. Norton.

2. Black, R., 2019. *Glossophobia (Fear of Public Speaking): Are you Glossophobic?.* [Online] Available at: https://www.psycom.net/glossophobia-fear-of-public-speaking [Accessed 2021].

3. Chamorro-Premuzic, T., 2020. *How to Spot an Incompetent Leader.* [Online] Available at: https://hbr.org/2020/03/how-to-spot-an-incompetent-leader [Accessed 7 September 2021].

4. Martin, S. & Marks, J., 2019. *Messengers: Who We Listen To, Who We Don't, and Why.* London: Random House Books.

CHAPTER FOUR: The Audience – Point A

1. Duarte, N., 2012. *HBR Guide to Persuasive Presentations.* Boston: Harvard Business Review Press.

2. Covey, S. R., 1989. *The Seven Habits of Highly Effective People: Restoring the character ethic.* New York: Simon and Schuster.

CHAPTER SEVEN: The Open and Close

1. Brown, B., 2010. *TEDx Houston: The Power of Vulnerability.* [Online] Available at: https://www.ted.com/talks/brene_brown_the_power_of_vulnerability [Accessed 2021].

2. Grant, A., 2014. *How I Overcame the Fear of Public Speaking.* [Online] Available at: https://www.psychologytoday.com/nz/blog/give-and-take/201409/how-i-overcame-the-fear-public-speaking [Accessed 2021].

CHAPTER EIGHT: Your Core Content

1. Tversky, A. & Kahneman, D., 1985. The Framing of Decisions and the Psychology of Choice. *Behavioral Decision Making.*

2. Kahneman, D. & Lovallo, D., 2003. *Delusions of Success: How Optimism Undermines Executives' Decisions.* [Online] Available at: https://hbr.org/2003/07/delusions-of-success-how-optimism-undermines-executives-decisions

3. McKee, R., 1997. *Story: substance, structure, style, and the principles of screenwriting.* New York: Harper Collins Publishers.

4. Harari, Y. N., 2011. *Sapiens: A Brief History of Humankind.* London: Penguin Random House.

5. King, S., 2020. *On Writing: A memoir of the craft.* Reissue ed. New York: Scribner.

6. Robinson, K., 2006. *TED: Do Schools Kill Creativity?.* [Online] Available at: https://www.ted.com/talks/sir_ken_robinson_do_schools_kill_creativity?language=en [Accessed 2021].

CHAPTER NINE: Visual Aids

1. Tufte, E. R., 2003. *PowerPoint is Evil.* [Online] Available at: https://www.wired.com/2003/09/ppt2/ [Accessed 2021].

2. Medina, J., 2014. *Brain rules: 12 principles for surviving and thriving at work, home and school.* 2nd ed. Seattle: Pear Press.

3. Godin, S., 2007. *Seth's Blog: Really Bad Powerpoint.* [Online] Available at: https://seths.blog/2007/01/really_bad_powe/ [Accessed 2021].

4. Ibid

5. Duarte, N., 2008. *Slide:ology.* Sebastopol, CA: O'Reilly Media.

6. Duarte, N., 2012. *HBR Guide to Persuasive Presentations.* Boston: Harvard Business Review Press.

CHAPTER ELEVEN: Courage

1. Weissman, J., 2009. *The Power Presenter.* Hoboken, New Jersey: John Wiley & Sons.

2. Ireland, T., 2014. *What Does Mindfulness Meditation Do to Your Brain?.* [Online] Available at: https://blogs.scientificamerican.com/guest-blog/what-does-mindfulness-meditation-do-to-your-brain/ [Accessed 2020].

3. Ibid

4. Suzuki, W., 2017. *The Brain-changing Benefits of Exercise.* [Online] Available at: https://www.ted.com/talks/ wendy_suzuki_the_brain_changing_benefits_of_exercise/ transcript#t-10480

5. Grant, A., 2014. *How I Overcame the Fear of Public Speaking.* [Online] Available at: https://www.psychologytoday.com/nz/ blog/give-and-take/201409/how-i-overcame-the-fear-public-speaking [Accessed 2021].

6. Ibid

7. Weissman, J., 2009. *The Power Presenter.* Hoboken, New Jersey: John Wiley & Sons.

CHAPTER TWELVE: Connect

1. Weissman, J., 2009. *The Power Presenter.* Hoboken, New Jersey: John Wiley & Sons

2. Rodenburg, P., 1991. *The Right to Speak: A journey through the voice.* London: Methuen Drama.

3. Rodenburg, P., 2008. *The Second Circle.* New York: W. W. Norton.

Praise for Step into the Spotlight

From the presentation maestro himself, Russell Pickering's book Step into the Spotlight is a must read for anyone wanting to improve their presentation skills. It's like Russell is having a conversation with you, anticipating all those questions and worries you have about giving presentations – and then soothingly, skilfully explaining how to address them. The book is filled with practical tools and tips, clear graphics and actionable takeaways. Backed up by research and his wealth of experience, I also love how Russell includes some of his own presentation mis-steps and learnings to illustrate key points!

Suzi McAlpine, leadership coach and author of *Beyond Burnout: How to Spot it, Stop it and Stamp it Out*

I'm pleased to endorse this new book from Russell in which he gives thoughtful, inciteful and practical advice on how to present effectively in both real and virtual environments. From communicating with connection and persuasion, turning data into insights, telling stories to inspire others, to the practicalities of knowing your brief, timing and setting, even the importance of understanding framing, lighting and sound – Russell covers it all in his practical, easy to follow way.'

Martin Wiseman, Country Managing Partner,
DLA Piper New Zealand

What a terrific read! Clear, relevant and beautifully engaging, Step into the Spotlight will give any potential speaker the confidence and courage to construct and deliver an authentic, engaging and effective speech - and importantly, one that connects in a meaningful way to the audience. Highly recommended.

Jennifer Ward-Lealand CNZM - actor, director, previous New Zealander of the Year

A great book which can help everyone with their presentations. Entertaining and informative. Following Russell's advice will make a real difference for every presenter!

Wayne McNee, Founder and Principal, Wayne McNee Consulting Limited

From the start, the emphasis on authenticity as a power, particularly in these times of 'tectonic shifts', resonated. In my work I regularly see great ideas struggling to be communicated. Following the guide provided in Step into the Spotlight will help bridge the communication gap that can exist between creation and execution.

We learn that a persuasive presentation does not need to come at the sacrifice of authenticity.

As someone who still gets hot, sweaty and a bit panicky about presentations, the focus on respecting the audience is a key mindset shift. Audiences will thank you for using this book!

Lucie Drummond, GM Sustainability, Mercury

I found Step into the Spotlight much better than some other presentation how-to books because of the attention the author pays to often-missed practical details as he supports the reader through the presenting cycle from preparation, delivery and post-performance learnings. It's an impressive guide, written in a non-showy, warm and engaging style. With easy-to-remember chapter summaries and specific advice given to virtual presentations, this is a fresh and pragmatic take on learning a skill that we all want to do more of effortlessly (or at least appear like it is!).

Adrienne Bonell, leadership coach, independent director